CONSTRUCTING LIVED EXPERIENCES

Constructing Lived Experiences

Representations of black mothers in child
sexual abuse discourses

CLAUDIA BERNARD
Goldsmiths College, University of London

Ashgate

Aldershot • Burlington USA • Singapore • Sydney

Published by
Ashgate Publishing Limited
Gower House
Croft Road
Aldershot
Hampshire GU11 3HR
England

Ashgate Publishing Company
131 Main Street
Burlington, VT 05401-5600 USA

Ashgate website: http://www.ashgate.com

British Library Cataloguing in Publication Data
Bernard, Claudia
    Constructing lived experiences : representations of black
    mothers in child sexual abuse discourses. -
    (Interdisciplinary research series in ethnic, gender and
    class relations)
    1. Child sexual abuse 2.Children, Black
    I.Title
    362.7'6'0896

Library of Congress Control Number: 2001090206

ISBN 1 84014 938 8

Printed in Great Britain by
Antony Rowe Ltd, Chippenham, Wiltshire

Contents

Acknowledgements

The process from research to book has been a long and challenging one, and the numerous people who contributed support along the way have made this book possible. Foremost, I would like to thank the women who courageously shared their stories and experiences with me. I am deeply grateful to these women who gave so much of themselves in the interviews. I would also like to thank those individuals, agencies and groups who assisted me in locating women to interview. I thank the Research Committee, Goldsmiths College, University of London, for providing the funds for me to complete my research. I would especially like to thank the British Sociological Association Violence Against Women Study Group, who provided a supportive space for me to explore some of my ideas for this book. Close friends Khalida Khan and Pam Menzies contributed both concrete and emotional support in numerous ways during the research and writing of this book. Also, Peter Lachman was most generous in providing creative and emotional space in Maine, USA, where many of my ideas for this book crystallised, and again in South Africa, which energised me for working on the last two chapters of this book. I particularly thank him for his generosity. I am most indebted to Christine Nugent for her intellectual and emotional support, and general encouragement during this project. I especially thank her for reading and commenting on several chapters of this book. I am also grateful to Danielle Turney for her insightful comments on portions of this book, also for our many conversations over the years that have informed some of my thinking. My sister, Heather Bernard, and cousin, Dawn Walton, provided general support throughout and are a good source of strength. My editors have been patient along the way and I wish to thank them for seeing this project through to completion. Finally, I am especially grateful to my partner, David Katz, whose endless amount of support, love, and encouragement sustained me during the process of writing this book.

1 Introduction

Aims of the Book

This book is centrally concerned with representations of black mothers in child sexual abuse discourses. Prevailing paradigms of intrafamilial child sexual abuse proffer ideas of the "collusive mother" that exert a powerful influence on intervention strategies in child protection cases. In challenging such ideas, a critical starting point of this book is that whilst all mothers of abused children may have some common experiences, divisions constructed around race and social class create a very different set of circumstances within which they respond to the abuse of their children. In centring attention on black mothers' experiences, I argue that to fully understand their reactions and responses necessitates an examination of their lived experiences within its broader social context. Through a critical discussion of the nature of mother-blame in child sexual abuse discourses, I seek to illuminate the specificity of black mothers' situations whilst critically assessing the structural, cultural and emotional factors that interplay for them. By providing an exploration of the links between race and gender as important markers for experience, I employ the intersectionality paradigm to call attention to the notion that black mothers occupy a range of multiple and contradictory positions that have implications for their help-seeking and protective strategies in the aftermath of abuse.

Thus, a central concern of the book is to explore the experience of child sexual abuse within black families to develop paradigms that are grounded in knowledge of black mothers' lived experiences. The focus on black women as mothers acknowledges that they are usually the designated carers with primary responsibilities for bringing up children. As a consequence, they are usually the parents left to deal with child protection services in the aftermath of abuse. Utilising data drawn from interviews conducted with black mothers whose children had been sexually abused, this book seeks to interrogate through the lens of black feminist thinking how race and gender dynamics shape black mothers' responses. It is my contention that in order to deepen understandings of how black mothers' responses to the sexual victimisation of their children are constructed and negotiated, the racially gendered dimensions of their experiences require examination to elucidate how multiple oppressions cohere for them.

1

Rationale for the Book

The stimulus for this book derives from my first-hand experiences of working with mothers as a child protection social worker in the statutory sector. I was struck then by the extent of mother-blame that overwhelmingly characterised social work intervention with families where child sexual abuse occurred. At the same time, I observed that mothers' responses to the abuse of their children were repeatedly represented as attributes of their parenting abilities. Most significantly, in our society where mothers primarily are the main carers of children, whether sexual abuse is intrafamilial or extrafamilial they are the parent who is most likely to encounter social welfare agencies and whose parenting most comes up for an intensive scrutiny. Therefore, whether consciously or unconsciously, professional helpers always managed to shift the burden of responsibility on to mothers and proffered the prevailing view of mothers' culpability in the abuse of their children. I found that one of the hardest attitudes to break down was the deeply entrenched belief that mothers were complicit in the abuse of their children. But perhaps most damaging of all is that underlying the claim of mothers as collusive is the assumption that they are actively or passively complicit in the abuse of their children; they were thus often charged with failing to protect. In particular, I was surprised and alarmed at the way in which professional helpers employed the collusive paradigm and rarely questioned the notion of gendered power relations as an important construct in discourses of child sexual abuse.

Whilst these ideas were rarely explicitly articulated, their influence nonetheless had profound effects in shaping a discourse of mothers as collusive and, more importantly, subjected their parenting to a negative scrutiny. I soon learnt that presumptions of the collusive mother were so deeply ingrained in professional discourses that old patterns of thinking were difficult to shift. Perhaps not surprisingly, there was resistance to any perspective that was rooted in an understanding of gendered power relations between men and women in families as a way of beginning to conceptualise mothers' responses to the sexual abuse of their children. Attempting to explode the many misconceptions that informed practice with mothers brought into sharp focus the ways in which normative assumptions about mothers and fathers' roles in the family actively shaped professional judgements about mothers and gave rise to a particular oppressive practice with mothers. What was most apparent was that embedded gender-biased assumptions about mothers' roles are among the most difficult and challenging aspects of thinking about sexual abuse in families. It felt to me almost as if any attempt to disrupt the taken for granted assumptions that it is mothers' sole responsibility to safeguard the welfare of their children inevitably brought the charge of over-identifying with mothers and losing focus of the children concerned.

At the same time, my disquiet at the levels of mother-blaming provoked my growing unease at the lack of understanding of the particular experiences of mothers from black and minority ethnic groups. I was especially alarmed by the casual reliance on explanations that rested on assumptions of culture-centred suppositions to explain child sexual abuse in black and minority ethnic families. Significantly, the interwoveness and interconnectedness of race, gender, and socio-economic factors as part of the social fabric in which black mothers are situated and the implications for their responses to the sexual victimisation of their children is underrepresented in the literature and in conceptualisation. What seemed apparent to me is that intervention practices that rested on normative assumptions of black mothers' parenting abilities would fail to recognise the powerful interacting forces that cohere for them to bring a particular response to their children's victimisation. Such an approach would be limited for considering the realities for black mothers and ultimately will fail to engage them in any meaningful way. My thinking then was underpinned by a perspective that suggests that a culture-specific standpoint is not only imbued with an ethnocentrism but masks a deeper problem of racism in the construction of black families in welfare discourses. My thinking is still the same now, though I have come to see the importance of opening up questions of how cultural meanings and values of child-rearing and parenting practices are understood in black and ethnic minority families for the development of culturally competent intervention. Equally important is the need to consider where interventions predicated on suppositions of cultural relativism may obscure the workings of oppressive and abusive practices to black women and children in their families (Baylis and Downie, 1997).

Perhaps most critically for me, because the thinking about black mothers was not grounded in an understanding of their lived experiences, intervention served to reflect and reproduce existing powerlessness with this group of mothers and inevitably deepened their distress and exacerbated the stigma felt by these mothers. In retrospect, I now recognise more clearly my struggles to reconcile the conflict I felt in my values and perspective; most notably, the challenges posed in being part of a system that reproduced the oppression these mothers experienced in their families through an intervention that rested on assumptions of the "collusive mother". In many respects, the point at which these issues crystallised for me was in gaining a deeper understanding of the consequences of an anti-oppressive social work approach. Intervention strategies are needed that will make a qualitative and sustainable difference for assisting mothers to respond to the needs of their children in the aftermath of child sexual abuse victimisation and to enable them to participate fully in any child protection investigations from a position of strength. I therefore became most interested in developing a perspective of how racism and gender oppression prohibits an open exploration of painful issues surrounding abuse and maltreatment in black families. Most importantly, interrogation of these issues provides us with the means to begin to conceptualise black mothers' responses for expanding theoretical frameworks to facilitate effective responses to black families.

Against this background I was motivated to open up questions that would contribute to a deeper understanding of the multiplicity of factors that impact on black mothers' responses to their children's sexual abuse. Against this background, I was motivated to undertake research into the nature of black mothers' experiences, to make visible their struggles to cope with the abuse of their children in the context of contradictions and ambiguities. Thus, the research that is the basis for this book focused on black mothers' experiences and understandings of the sexual abuse of their children. Drawing on first-hand accounts of black mothers, the research examines the way race and gender coalesce to inform black mothers' help-seeking and protective strategies on discovery of the abuse of their children. A principal aim of the research is to explore the uncharted territory of black mothers' accounts to candidly bring their experiences into full view. Another aim is to generate data to extend and deepen our understandings of the complexities involved for black mothers in making sense of the abuse of their children and giving voice to those experiences. In Britain, there is currently a paucity of original research and theoretical literature on child sexual abuse in black families. In addressing this under-explored area, my goal is to offer a perspective to promote practice with black mothers that is firmly located in the lived experiences of mothers themselves. Perhaps, most importantly, this book develops understandings that could be drawn upon to inform child protection policy and practice to ultimately enhance strategies for helping in black families.

Overview of the Book

In chapter two I address the theoretical and conceptual framework underpinning the book. I give an overview of feminist paradigms of the representation of mothers in child sexual abuse discourses and praxis. Drawing on a broad spectrum of perspectives, I review current research to consider how culturally embedded ideas of mothers as collusive are reinforced and reproduced in children protection practices. The discussion elucidates the strengths and limitations in the literature on mothers, then moves on to consider the specificity of black mothers' position within broader debates about child sexual abuse in black families. In chapter three I set out the research methodology and discuss the conceptual framework that has guided the study and discuss some of the ethical issues that have framed the data gathering and analysis. The remainder of the book presents the findings of the research to explore a number of key areas. Chapter four draws on the findings to examine the emotional and behavioural responses of mothers to unravel the multiple determining factors that influenced their responses. Using the voices of mothers to illustrate particular points, the paradigm of divided loyalty is employed as a conceptual framework for analysing the complexity of mothers' emotional responses. The multi-layered nature of their experiences in their families and communities are examined to argue that the nature of the relationship between black mothers and their families are key determinants of their responses. Chapter five discusses the effects of the abuse on women's mothering. Here I draw on data gathered from both mothers who did and did not involve child protection services to argue that the processes by which mothers made such decisions are imbued with a set of contradictions and ambiguities. Particularly, I address the centrality of mothers' coping mechanisms, and the meanings they attach to their mothering and support networks to explore their parenting in the aftermath of abuse. Chapter six focuses on mothers' help-seeking to address issues surrounding risk assessment for black children in the aftermath of abuse. I draw out some of the main messages from the research to assess the implications for black mothers' help-seeking behaviour for the safety and emotional needs of their children. Through some reflections on the nature of mothers' experiences, the implications of risk factors for black children are explored. In particular, I examine how mothers' perceptions of the child protection services influence their decisions on whether and how to involve helping professionals. The book concludes by outlining a framework for working with black mothers and develops the argument that non-abusing mothers can play a key role in contributing to their children's recovery from abuse. Mapping out the tensions inherent in balancing the needs of mothers against the needs and rights of black children, this final chapter explores from a standpoint rooted in anti-oppressive values, the complexities and dilemmas involved in professional practice for working collaboratively with mothers to promote the welfare of their children.

2 Setting the Scene: Representations of Mothers in Child Sexual Abuse Discourses

This chapter explores representations of mothers in child sexual abuse discourse and practice. Arguably, feminist and pro-feminist interpretations are at the forefront of critiquing mother-blaming theories, and are transforming the thinking of mothers in child sexual abuse discourses. By centrally addressing gender as a locus of power relations, scholars writing from a feminist perspective have not only been careful to draw a sharp distinction between abusing and non-abusing parents, but have also distinguished between mothers and fathers in their analysis of child sexual abuse in the home. More recently, first-person accounts from mothers of abused children and original research with mothers are bringing their voices to the public domain, and are challenging the many misconceptions that abound about the "collusive mother" (Ashley, 1992; Dempster, 1993; Hooper, 1992; Johnson, 1992; Skinner, 2000). In particular, first-person accounts by mothers shift our focus on to the devastating impact of sexual abuse by someone loved and trusted and bring into sharp focus that they experience a number of problems and have their own needs. An important starting point therefore is how we understand the role of mothers who in the majority of cases are the non-abusing parent, and whom children largely depend on for support and protection in the aftermath of abuse.

A review of the literature on child sexual abuse shows that there are significant gender differences in the way mothers and fathers are represented in child protection discourse and practice (Bell, 1993; Birns and Meyer, 1993; Breckenridge and Baldry, 1997; Caplan, 1990; Corby, 1996; Elbow and Mayfield, 1991; Faller, 1988; Garvey, Florence, Pezaro and Tan, 1990; Gilgun, 1984; Hooper, 1997; Hooper and Humphreys, 1997; Mittler, 1997; Parton, 1998; Skinner, 2000; Trotter, 1997; Wattenberg, 1985). These perspectives have pointed to the way arguments about mothers' complicity in their children's abuse moves the responsibility for the abuse away from men and attributes blame to mothers

7

(DeYoung, 1994; Hooper, 1992; Johnson, 1992). Those committed to placing gender at the centre of their analyses are keenly aware that mothers figure centrally in responsibility for abuse, and that fathers are largely absent by their invisibility in both practice and research (Farmer and Owen, 1998; Hooper, 1992; Milner, 1993). This prominence is indicated in the prevalence of research that consistently cites fathers, stepfathers, male relatives and other men as overwhelmingly the perpetrators of sexual abuse against children. Nonetheless, there is still a tendency in research and practice to give greater attention to mothers' supposed "failure to protect" rather than to focus on men's abusive behaviour (Farmer and Owen, 1998; Hooper and Humphreys, 1998). Indeed, the attention given to fathers or father-figures in the literature on risk and child protection is noticeably absent, and work with families tends to focus largely on mothers and female care-givers (Green, 1996; Hooper, 1992; Krane and Davies, 2000; Milner, 1996; O'Hagan, 1997; Oko, 2000; Pringle, 1998). Though legally both parents may have responsibility for the safety and protection of children, the fact remains that it is women as mothers who routinely come up for an intense scrutiny and who most encounter the negative attention of child protection agencies. Consequently, the gaze is deflected away from men and firmly focused on mothers, thus reinforcing the prevailing assumption within dominant discourses of child welfare that it is women as mothers who are assumed to have primary responsibility for children's well-being. Subsequently, when anything goes wrong in the family, it is mothers' parenting that comes up for an intense professional scrutiny (Milner, 1993).

Feminist analyses have called attention to the complex processes involved for mothers in the aftermath of intra-familial child sexual abuse, and have long recognised that emotional and social processes are critical in shaping mothers' responses (Carter, 1993; Green, 1996; Hooper, 1992; Jacobs, 1994; McIntre, 1981; Myer, 1985; Sirles and Frank, 1989). In her insightful text "Victimised Daughters: Incest and the Development of the Female Self", Jacobs summarises some of the main theoretical formulations on mothers to outline the dominant explanatory frameworks used to explain mothers' positions in child sexual abuse paradigms. She identifies three dominant models to explain mothers' predicaments: "The mother as colluder; the mother as helpless dependent; and the mother as victim herself" (p.26). These approaches all emphasise mothers' powerlessness in protecting their children from abuse. What has been highlighted most succinctly by feminist research is that on the disclosure of

8

sexual abuse, the cognitive, emotional and relational world of mothers is shattered (Cammaert, 1988; Dempster, 1993; Hooper, 1992; Johnson, 1992; Myer, 1985). In addition, feminists have stressed that issues of power and gender relations in families are critical to an understanding of their impact on mothers' psychological, emotional and behavioural responses (Dempster, 1993; Hooper, 1992; MacLeod and Saraga, 1988; Nelson, 1985; Print and Dey, 1992; Smith, 1994). This is in contrast to the portrayal of mothers in dominant child sexual abuse discourse, which typically characterise them as collusive, cold, frigid, emotionally distant, and being in denial (Bell, 1993; Green, 1996; Jacobs, 1994; Nelson, 1987; Salt, Myer, Colman and Sauzier, 1990; Surrey, 1991). Nelson, for instance, provides an excellent review of the literature depicting mothers as collusive, and her analysis debunks the many myths and misconceptions surrounding representation of mothers in child sexual abuse. What is highlighted most powerfully is how dominant explanatory frameworks fail to explore the way women who may be economically and emotionally dependent on their children's abusers may perceive their choices. Green (1996), exploring the construction of mothers in incest, illustrates the complexities of the issues by pointing out that mothers' responses will be determined by the extent of power relations within the family, and are augmented by the emotional, social and financial stresses that they face.

The importance of understanding the effects of abuse on mothers' internal sense of self and world is critical for providing the right kind of intervention (Ashley, 1992; Green, 1996; Scott, 1996). Moreover, it is important to recognise that suspecting their husbands or partners of abuse will damage mothers' internal world constructs, and such damage is a major contributory factor in influencing their agency and actions (Green, 1996; Hooper and Humphreys, 1998). Essentially, how mothers see themselves, how they see their relationships with their partners, and most importantly, how they see their roles and their options, will certainly all be affected.

Some commentators argue that especially where the abuser is the woman's husband or partner, learning of the abuse can elicit a powerful grief response in mothers such as shock, numbness, denial, fear, anxiety, guilt, anger and depression (Ashley, 1992; Green, 1996; Johnson, 1992). In particular, first hand accounts of those who work directly with mothers of abused children emphasise that some mothers may have no knowledge of the abuse, others may not have picked up the "clues" surrounding abuse, whilst others may know about it but might be fearful of seeking help

9

(Hildebrand, 1989).

Moreover, as research has identified, some mothers may not be in a position to protect their children when their male partners are violent (Farmer and Owen, 1998; Hester and Pearson, 1998; Truesdell, McNeil, Deschner, 1986). For example, in their study of forty-four children whose names had been placed on the child protection register, Farmer and Owen found that where children were being sexually abused, in two-fifths of cases the mother was also experiencing domestic violence. Hester and Pearson's (1998) study echoes the findings of Farmer and Owen. In looking at the interconnected nature of child abuse and domestic violence, they found that domestic violence occurred in more than half of the thirty-seven case files reviewed where children had been identified, as being sexually abused by a father or father-figure was the main focus of concern for child protection workers. An important message to be drawn from these research findings is that when working with child abuse professionals should always be alerted to the possibilities of domestic violence and its impact on mothers' ability to parent effectively to protect their children.

Nonetheless, in the absence of taking immediate action to report the abuse or leave their partners it can be construed by professional helpers that a mother is collusive or complicit in some way. Corby (1996) notes that professionals' judgements about the attitude of the non-abusing parent to the alleged perpetrator are significant in informing social work intervention with mothers. For example, if mothers do not leave abusive men, or are ambivalent about their feelings towards their partners, this can often be interpreted as their complicity in the abuse. Growing evidence from a number of recent studies that have focused more specifically on the testimonies of mothers of abused children provides useful empirical data of mothers' perspectives and challenges theoretical formulations attributing blame to mothers (Hooper, 1992; Dempster, 1993; Johnson, 1992). For example, in "Mothers Surviving Sexual Abuse", Hooper (1992) draws on original research with mothers to examine the multi-faceted processes that interplay to influence their emotional and behavioural responses. She notes in particular those women whose children are abused by their husband or partner are posed with a number of challenges in their decision-making and help-seeking. Hooper found that on discovery of abuse, some mothers were rendered unable to make immediate decisions and were left with an overwhelming sense of guilt and shame. She also found that few women were immediately able to adopt a position of rejection of the offender. In particular, it is contended that women are more likely to be deterred from leaving an abusive man if they feel themselves to be financially or emotionally dependent on them (Hooper, 1992).

In sum, the existing body of work exploring the representation of mothers in child sexual abuse discourses has undoubtedly dismantled some of the deep-rooted assumptions about mothers and raised questions about gender roles. Focusing on issues of gendered power relations as a starting point, feminist perspectives challenge the presumptions upon which notions of mothers are rested to bring new insights into the complexities of their situation. Perhaps most importantly, feminist theorists have problematised gender from the standpoint of power relations and have interrogated the unfavourable position of mothers. Undoubtedly, their most substantial critique is that implicit valuation and normative judgements about traditional female roles are embedded in child protection discourse. In contesting prevailing notions of mothers as collusive, feminists have ensured that conscious and unconscious assumptions about family and gender roles are not left unchallenged. In so doing, they call attention to the notion that ideas about mothers are based on clinical hypotheses, abstract formulations premised upon certain sexist and culturally biased assumptions that are often unsupported by empirical research (MacLeod and Saraga, 1988).

However, a close reading of the feminist literature on mothers reveals a paucity of analysis exploring the specificity of black mothers' experiences. Much of feminist scholarship on mothers has focused on the importance of gendered power relations and less on the significance of race as it intersects with gender. The priorities and concerns for black mothers are either excluded or marginalised from feminist explorations of mothers. A criticism that could be levelled against much feminist work on mothers is that they have typically focused on the experiences of white mothers, from which generalisations are then made to all mothers. This lack of attention suggests there is an implicit assumption in the existing feminist analyses of homogeneity of experiences. Black mothers' exclusion and marginalisation from debates means the particular problems that they face have not been fully explored in feminist accounts of mothers. There may be strong parallels and similarities between all mothers, but suffice it to say that the very different conditions of women's lives operate to shape lived experiences. Therefore, black mothers' experiences may differ because of their social location. Specifically, gender and race are inextricably linked for black women, and are important dimensions influencing the way individual meaning is constructed (Hill Collins, 1998). Significantly, race

11

will not only influence attitudes towards black mothers, but will profoundly frame how black mothers' gendered experiences shape their choices and help-seeking actions in the aftermath of the abuse of their children. Clearly, an exploration of the simultaneity of race and gender oppression is fundamental to understanding the complexities involved for black mothers' responses and actions.

Child Sexual Abuse in Black Families

A discussion of black mothers' reactions to the abuse of their children must be located within broader debates about child sexual abuse in black families and communities. A careful examination should be undertaken of a number of key issues that are important and controversial. Three points concern me here. Firstly, little attention has so far been paid to the specific issue of sexual abuse in black families (Butt and Mirza, 1996). Currently there is a paucity of original research and theoretical work on sexual abuse with a specific focus on black families. Accurate data on the incidence and prevalence of child sexual abuse in black families is not easy to come by, and this poses a major problem in having a sense of the true scale of the problem in black communities (Jackson, 1996; Mtezuka, 1996; Pierce and Pierce, 1987; Wilson, 1993). It is contended that a good deal of sexual abuse is not reported to official agencies such as the police or social services departments, and thus does not appear on official registers (Bernard, 1998; Wilson, 1993).

One of the major problems associated with the reporting of sexual abuse in black families is that there can be a great deal of fear and mistrust of statutory agencies (Mtezuka, 1996; Wyatt, 1990). Furthermore, black people may feel alienated from the whole notion of law enforcement (Mama, 1993; Mtzeuka, 1996). Moreover, sexual abuse is not discussed openly for fear of exposing the black community to coercive intervention by statutory agencies (Jackson, 1996; Wilson, 1993). The threatening nature of a topic like child sexual abuse may make some people hesitant to seek outside help. If the black child is abused within their family, it becomes especially traumatic and can be almost impossible for the child to disclose to outsiders what is happening to them (Droisen, 1989; Jackson, 1996). Black children from a very early age experience racism, and a cushioning of the effects of racism is usually undertaken within the family network. Here black children are particularly dependent for support on networks of family, and this may make it particularly difficult for them to disclose. For example, telling about the abuse may not be safe for children, and they may feel they are betraying their families. As hooks (1989) has so cogently argued: "so many black people have been raised to believe that there is just so much that you should not talk about, not in private and not in public" (p.21). Thus, analyses of child sexual abuse in black communities must be grounded in an understanding of how racism presents a hindrance for black children to tell. The reporting of sexual abuse in black communities generates fear of reprisals, and could incur marginalisation or even exclusion from families and communities (Bernard, 1997). It is accepted by large numbers in the black community that there will be little justice in the criminal justice system and as a result black people are less confident that their concerns will be taken seriously when they are the victims of crimes (Mama, 1993).

The second factor of importance is that the possibility of black men's involvement in the sexual abuse of their own children opens up painful and difficult issues for black women. An area of concern for many is that negative and distorted messages about black men are conveyed to us through the media and other social institutions (Mercer and Julien, 1988). It is suggested that the dominant representations of black men emphasise a view of them as feckless, absent fathers. Additionally, black male sexuality is represented as wanton and bestial (Smith, 1998). To some degree, the negative stereotypes of black men act to shape the way they are responded to, and may reinforce the general racism directed against black men in their dealings with welfare agencies (Arshad, 1996; Bryan, Dadzie and Scarfe, 1985). Moreover, it is suggested that in a context where the state plays a significant role in the demonisation of black men, for black women to raise the issue of their violence and abusive behaviour in public is to invite a racist backlash (Mama, 1995; Mtzeuka, 1996; Wilson, 1993). To name the reality would mean confronting difficult questions that would evoke strong feelings within black communities, as well as dealing with the possibility of a racist interpretation (Wilson, 1993). It could be argued that the more marginalised the group, the more likely they will be to strive to protect their image (Richie, 1996). Given these sets of circumstances, perhaps not surprisingly, there is a reluctance to engage publicly with the issue of childhood sexual abuse in black communities, and a general resistance to addressing the problem.

Thirdly, the representation of black families in welfare debates offers some explanation into how perceptions of them might inform responses to black families in general and black mothers in particular (Boushel, 2000). It is argued by anti-racist thinkers that state apparatuses such as social work are mired in assumptions about race, and play a critical role in reproducing the ideology of "inferior" black families (see Lawrence, 1982 for a fuller exploration of the way sociological perspectives pathologise and problematise black families). The defining factor, according to some commentators is that the negative construction of black families fosters the devaluation of child-rearing practices and caregiving in black families and communities (Ahmad, 1990; Robinson, 1995). In general, anti-racist scholars have sought to reveal the way certain images and ideas about black families have become an integral part of welfare ideology and practice, to show how such assumptions influence judgements of what constitutes good enough parenting in black families. According to Carby (1992), "rather than a concern to protect or preserve the black family in Britain, the state reproduced common-sense notions of its inherent pathology" (p.219). Anti-racist thinkers note that by applying an Anglo-centrically focused lens as the standard by which to judge what constitutes a good family, the state implicitly relies on a deficit model of black families that depicts them as failures (Phoenix, 1990). In particular, they emphasise that a deficit model fails to consider the survival techniques utilised by black families in the face of adversity. By implicitly using the experiences of white nuclear middle-class families as normative, the state reinforces a particular image of white middle-class motherhood against which all mothers are judged, and in the process has pathologised black motherhood as deficient. Assumptions about good enough mothering make it more likely, it could be argued, that if you are a black and working class mother, you will be more liable to be a target for state surveillance. Thus, it is suggested that black people may not necessarily see professional helpers as protectors of their communities, but may indeed see them as reinforcing oppression.

Analyses of the way black families are represented in welfare debates offer some scope for us to consider how black mothers construct meaning in the context of sexual abuse in their families. Likewise, they can help us to consider the implications for black women's help-seeking as well as their perceptions of statutory agencies' likely responses in the aftermath of abuse (Bryan, Dadzie and Scarfe, 1985; Carby, 1982; Mama, 1996). By underscoring the importance of race in shaping the construction of welfare, anti-racist analyses bring into sharper focus that black families often receive an inadequate or negative response from helping agencies when they are experiencing stress and difficulties. It is suggested that this is reflected most visibly in the over-representation of black people in the control aspects of welfare services (Chand, 2000; Jones, 1994; Phillips, 1995). For example, there is evidence to show that black people are over-represented in mental health services (Fernando, 1995), there are disproportionate numbers of black children in the public care system (Barn, 1993; Beddington and Miles, 1989; Luthera, 1997; Butt and Mirza, 1996), and black women are over-represented in prisons (Chigwada-Bailey, 1997).

Taking up questions of the complex ways race intersects with gender, black feminists have been most concerned to highlight that black women occupy a range of multiple and contradictory positions that have implications for their relationship to welfare agencies (Carby, 1982; Mama, 1996). Black feminists interrogate race from a standpoint that examines the intersection of gender, race and class to highlight the multifarious roles of women as mothers and as members of their families and communities. Most significantly, analyses from black feminist thinkers have illuminated the need to examine the gendered experiences of black mothers within the private sphere of their families, as well as their relationships to the public sphere to consider how these will profoundly influence their help-seeking behaviour.

An analysis of the intersecting effects of gender and race in black women's lives points to ways in which gender and power relations are embodied in black families, and identifies the complexities that are posed for black women and children in giving a voice to their experiences of violence and maltreatment (Mama, 1996). Black feminists' analyses usefully direct us towards an understanding of how the family is both a source of black women's strength as well as a source of their oppression (Carby, 1982). This contradictory position means it is a site of resistance, for example, in struggles against state racism .e.g. police racism and deaths in custody. Yet, ironically, it is also a site of oppression and poses dilemmas and challenges for black women in the aftermath of child sexual abuse and other forms of male violence in the home. Most significantly, an exploration of gender relations in black families and communities emphasises some of the contradictions for black women in their families, and the subsequent implications for their help-seeking behaviour in the aftermath of violence and abuse. Perhaps most importantly, the reality of male violence to black women and children in the family sits uneasily with the notion of the family as being a site of affirmation and resistance for black women.

These challenges notwithstanding, in endeavouring to emphasise the strengths of black families, there is a tendency to gloss over the issues of gender and unequal power relations that exist in such families. I would argue that an exploration of the gendered nature of black women and children's experiences in the family does not undermine or divert attention away from anti-racist analyses and initiatives. Rather, it strengthens them by bringing into sharper focus the different layers of experiences, giving us a much deeper understanding of the culturally gendered dimensions of black women's and girl's experiences in their families. Indeed, it is necessary to emphasise the strengths and resilience of black families to survive in a hostile environment, and to challenge the harmful stereotypes surrounding perceptions of black families. Notwithstanding, it is also important not to gloss over or obscure black women's and children's experiences of violence within their families. Such a stance not only colludes with abusive men, but also powerfully silences women and children from speaking publicly about the abuse and violence perpetrated by men in their families. Rather, the question should be at whose expense are we denying that sexual abuse occurs in black families? As Villorasa (1994) points out, "Silence only fuels the problem and leaves survivors feeling lost, confused, guilty and painfully alone" (p.520). Similarly, Kelly (1996) remarks that "Silence has been a major weapon in men's arsenal which has prevented women and children from talking about their experiences of sexual violence" (p.34). If we are not to loose sight of the rights of black children to be protected from sexual abuse, it is imperative that we interrogate the issues at play and find ways to explore the dynamics of sexual abuse, and thus break the silence surrounding the abuse of black children. Although there are risks in having an open discussion about child sexual abuse in black families, the risks of continuing to avoid such a discussion are even greater, because the consequence is that we leave a good number of black children in harmful and abusive situations.

Wilson (1993) proffers a black feminist analysis of the silence surrounding child sexual abuse in black families. Principally, she highlights the importance of race and gender to illuminate pervasive factors such as feelings of loyalty, shame, and fear of a racist backlash, that create a climate of silence around the subject of childhood sexual abuse in black families. As a consequence, she argues, the subject is surrounded by a wall of silence because of black women's alliances with black men and general feelings of responsibility to the black community. Wilson makes a compelling argument for understanding how the simultaneity of oppressions operates to contribute to secret keeping about child sexual abuse in black families. Moreover, racism not only affect mothers' abilities to hear their children's concerns, but also to access appropriate help through formal and informal processes to deal with the aftermath of child sexual abuse. Such an unravelling of the issues is important and indeed necessary if we are to identify and understand the complexities of child sexual abuse in black families. Ultimately, the racially gendered dimensions of black mothers' experiences require interrogation to elucidate how multiple oppressions intersect to bring a particular response to their children's victimisation.

3 The Research Methodology and Conceptual Framework

This chapter describes the methodological and conceptual framework that has guided the research. It is difficult to do justice to the range of methodological issues raised but a number of points that are inextricably linked are important to reflect upon to provide a context within which to understand the research. I will thus briefly describe the research under study and make some remarks about the research process before moving on to examine the methodological issues raised in recruiting respondents and gathering the data.

The central focus of the research was to conduct an inquiry into the perceptions and experiences of black mothers whose children have been sexually abused by someone in the family or someone known to them. Specifically, the research sought to understand black mothers' reactions by investigating how multiple oppressions impact on responses to child sexual abuse, and to investigate how mothers give voice to their experiences. Primarily, the research sought to examine the way race and gender coalesces to influence black mothers' help-seeking and protective strategies on discovery of the abuse. Thus, a principal aim of the research was to conduct a careful examination of the multi-layered interactions between black mothers, their children and families, and helping agencies in the aftermath of child sexual abuse. Another aim was to examine hidden assumptions, attitudes and beliefs to candidly bring the experiences of black mothers into full view to develop a deeper understanding of mothers' help-seeking strategies.

In pursuit of these aims, the research utilised a conceptual framework embedded in paradigms of intersectionality and was guided by the following questions: What were the concerns and dilemmas for black mothers when their children have been abused? What meanings did black mothers attach to their children's well-being and safety needs in the aftermath of child sexual abuse? What are mothers' perceptions of the effects of the abuse on their children? What are the effects of child sexual abuse on black mothers' relationships with their children? What factors influenced their decision-making on discovery of the abuse? What factors enabled or hindered them from taking protective action? What constitutes help and support for black mothers?

Study Design and Research Process

Drawing on a range of perspectives, the study design utilised a qualitative methodology of data collection and is underpinned by feminist epistemological approaches to research. There are some guiding principles that are at the heart of feminist research that were important to employ in the study. Notably, feminist researchers powerfully challenge research orthodoxies that reify claims to neutrality and objectivity, offering instead an alternative research paradigm that is rooted in an analysis of gendered power relationships (Fonow and Cook, 1991; Maynard and Purvis, 1994; Roberts, 1981). Above all, feminist research paradigms have been significant in opening up questions about the social relations involved in research production. In particular, feminists have explored the nature of power relations that are at the core of defining not only research questions, but also the research process and research outcomes (Mama, 1995; Reinharz, 1992). Perhaps, most importantly for me, feminist research is predicated on an analysis of the central importance of the relationship between the researcher and the researched and its impact on the data generated; it also emphasises the centrality of locating ourselves within our research (Moran-Ellis, 1995; Reay, 1996). Embedded in this principle is the thinking that researchers make transparent their epistemological position and bring a clear understanding of reflexivity in the research process (Reay, 1996). In this respect, these are some of the values and principles that my perspective is grounded in, and as such, feminist thinking had to be at the core of my research to guide the study.

In particular, black feminist researchers insist on the importance of an analysis of the intersection of race, gender, and class in the research processes and argue for a research paradigm grounded in these understandings (Mama, 1995; Marshall, 1994; Phoenix, 1994; Wheeler, 1994). Mama (1989) reminds us of the complex matrix of oppression black women experience, and perhaps most crucially, that the research process should not reproduce oppressive systems for respondents. Some of the potential benefits of such an approach were in recognising the importance of race and gender as interlocking cultural constructions that shape the lived experiences of the women I sought to study (Smith, 1998). Considering these factors helped me to keep in mind what the research experience might be like for the mothers. Importantly, as the group of mothers I intended to study experienced multiple forms of marginality, I needed to reflect critically on the research process to ensure that the respondents were not objectified or disempowered further by the research experience. In this respect, the frameworks I employed in the study draw heavily on a paradigm of intersectionality and provided me with a conceptual framework for guiding the research (Crenshaw, 1994; Hill Collins, 1998). The insights developed by black feminist thinkers around intersectionality have been valuable as a way forward for considering the subtleties of race and gender in the research experience. Specifically, I wanted to draw on research paradigms that enhanced my capacity to reflect on what I am doing (Seale, 1998), and reflexively look at the way my own values, beliefs, and perspectives translated into the research process. Thus, the insights of feminist and anti-racist researchers served as a powerful reminder for me to continually evaluate the ways my own social location and values affected the research process (Reay, 1996; Trinder, 2000) to consider ways to enhance the mothers' capacities to articulate their experiences from their own vantage points.

In developing a research framework for examining childhood sexual abuse in black families, it was important for me to address a number of methodological issues at different levels in the research process. A number of commentators have highlighted that there are many conceptual and methodological problems inherent in researching child sexual abuse (Barnet et al, 1997; Bradley and Lindsay, 1987; Finkelhor, 1986; Geffner, Rosenbaum, and Hughes, 1988; Ghate and Spencer, 1995; Herzberger, 1993; Kinard, 1985; Kinard, 1994; Levanthal, 1982; Russell, 1983; Westcott, 1996). The main concerns centre on the problems of defining and measuring child sexual abuse and the difficulties involved in obtaining accurate data. Finkelhor (1986) points out that researching child sexual abuse is beset by problems of inadequate samples, over simplistic research designs, conflicting definitions and unsophisticated analysis. It can therefore be surmised that obtaining accurate data on child sexual abuse is difficult in any case, because abuse is typically characterised by secrecy and denial, and within black families these factors are compounded by racism. It has to be acknowledged that much child sexual abuse does not come to the attention of persons outside the family, and even so a high number of the cases that are disclosed to outsiders never reach child protection services (Gomes-Schwartz, Horowitz and Cardarelli, 1990).

I was acutely aware that child sexual abuse in black families is difficult to study well because it is largely a hidden phenomenon (Caplan, 1998). Perhaps the major barrier to obtaining accurate data in childhood sexual abuse research in black communities is the under-reporting of the problem (Abney and Priest, 1995; Jackson, 1996; Mtezuka, 1996). Moreover, the problems associated with doing research on sexual abuse in black communities are compounded by the possibilities that the findings may be interpreted in ways to fuel societal racism about the scale of sexual abuse in black families (Mayall, 1991). Andersen, (1993) notes black people have more reason to be worried than white people that researchers conducting studies will exploit them. What has to be recognised is that one of the most crucial factors associated with gathering data on sexual abuse in black families is that there can be a great deal of fear and mistrust on the part of the respondents. The consequence of making a choice to speak to a researcher may mean that research participants could be ostracised by their peers (Patton, 1990, quoted in King 1996). Therefore, I could not underestimate how risky an act speaking to a researcher could be for some of the mothers. Thus, given the sensitive nature of the subject being studied, consideration of the context in which the research is taking place is vital, and I had to be alert to the levels of risk involved for participants that are already stigmatised and marginalised.

Negotiating Access to Sources of Data

The mothers were recruited through a variety of sources: mainly statutory and voluntary agencies with responsibilities for children and families social work and through publicity material distributed in health centres, GP surgeries and community-based projects working with black families and black women. To be eligible for the study, mothers had to have acknowledged that the sexual abuse had occurred and that they were not the perpetrators. The information sent to mothers specified what was meant by child sexual abuse. It was important to give a definition, as child sexual abuse is a complex social phenomenon to conceptualise, define and measure. For this reason, a broad definition of child sexual abuse was used: the involvement of dependant, developmentally immature children and adolescents in sexual activities, that they do not fully comprehend and to which they are unable to give informed consent (Driver, 1989). "Sexual behaviour may involve touching parts of the child or requesting the child to touch oneself, itself, or others; ogling the child in a sexual manner, taking

21

pornographic photographs, or requiring the child to look at parts of the body, observe sexual acts or other material in a way which is arousing to oneself' (Driver, 1989, p.3).

The sample was comprised of thirty self-selected mothers who described themselves as black British of African-Caribbean origin. I gathered from each participant biographical details concerning their age, marital status, occupation as well as information about their household composition. Thirteen of the participants were married or cohabiting with their male partners and seventeen were lone mothers, some with long-term partners not living in the same household. Participants ranged in age from twenty-four to forty-six (the mean age being thirty-five). Five of the mothers were employed in professional jobs, and eleven worked in service sector positions, mainly with low paying jobs. Twelve of the mothers were unemployed and on income support and two were full-time students. Six of the mothers were themselves recovering from childhood sexual abuse. A total of thirty-one children were involved, 30 girls and one boy (one mother had both her children, a son and daughter abused). The children ranged in age from six to fourteen.

All the children of the mothers who agreed to be in the study, had been abused by someone related to or acquainted with them, e.g. father or stepfather, mothers' boyfriends, relative, family friend, teacher or other trusted adult. However, only some of the mothers in the sample had reported the matter to child protection agencies. Discovery of the abuse had to have taken place at least six months before the interview. This approach was to allow for any child protection investigations that may have resulted from the disclosure, and also partly to be appreciative that immediately after discovery of abuse, families may be in crises that challenge their habitual coping patterns (Gomes-Schwartz, Horowitz and Cardarelli, 1990). It is suggested that it may not be appropriate for such families to be involved in research. Participation in the study was voluntary and the respondents were informed that they could withdraw at any time. All names and recognisable characteristics of the mothers and their children have been changed in the text so as to protect the anonymity of the women and their families.

From the outset of the research, I was confronted with a number of challenges and dilemmas, most specifically around gaining access to respondents. Perhaps the biggest potential problem that I faced involved how I was going to reach black women who matched the study criteria. With this thought in mind, I had to give much attention to how to present my project and myself not only to gatekeepers, but also to respondents (King, 1996). My first port of call was a number of local authority social services departments with core responsibilities for child protection work. I saw them as potential sites for identifying mothers to participate in the research and formally requested permission to approach their front-line workers who might have contact with mothers who matched the study criteria. I envisaged that these front-line workers would be able to identify suitable mothers whom I might recruit to participate in the study. I devised a leaflet giving brief details of the research goals and my background to answer questions and concerns that potential respondents might have had. I gave a letter and information about the research together with a statement of intent for practitioners to pass on to suitable mothers. I wanted potential respondents to have sufficient information to be able to understand what the research aims were and to be able to make informed choices about their participation. The information I sent out to gatekeepers thus explicitly stated the goals and objectives of the research and I clearly outlined the methods, values and theoretical orientation that framed the research questions. I also stipulated my own racialised and gendered identity as a black woman, and gave some details about my professional and academic background and the theoretical and practice grounding that I bring to the research. I envisaged that knowing that the researcher is another black woman might increase the possibility of potential participants being persuaded to take part in the study. For that reason I thought it important that I located myself and explicitly stated what personal and professional perspectives I would bring to the study. Principally, I wanted to allay concerns about any potential harm to, or exploitation of respondents as a result of the research experience.

Although I hoped that being explicit about my standpoint might encourage women to come forward, foremost in my thinking was that it might discourage some social services managers from involving their agencies in the study as a potential outcome of the research could be a critique of their professional practice. However, my approach proved to be protracted and I had not anticipated that gaining access to suitable participants would be so fraught with difficulties and involve so many layers of negotiation. I was invited along to meet senior childcare managers in a number of social services departments to discuss the study and was questioned at length about it. Whilst some declined to have their agencies involved, a great number were sympathetic to the research and allowed me access to their front-line workers. However, in cases where the

23

senior managers had given their permission for me to approach practitioners, I still had to enter into lengthy negotiations with a series of middle and first-line managers before I actually gained access to the practitioners who worked directly with mothers and thus held important gate-keeping functions. As with the senior managers, I also had to enter into lengthy negotiations with social work practitioners who were often reluctant to allow access to "their" clients. What is highlighted here is that access is a constantly negotiated process, rather than a one off event.

My original intention was to include mothers of Asian and African origin as part of the sample. No names were put forward by agencies I approached and I found it difficult to access such women who met the study criteria. Moreover, in the course of the study it became clear that the complexities involved in recruitment were ultimately too great to include them. Being an outsider, I found it much harder to make inroads into these communities and the pressure to move on to gain access to other sites was too great (Lee, 1993). While it is not impossible for an African-Caribbean researcher to gain access to Asian or African communities, I did not have the resources required to make this workable (i.e. my time and budget were limited and I had no access [or recourse] to the personnel necessary to facilitate interviewing women in their own language). Additionally, in reflecting on recruitment-related events, my efforts to access Asian and African women raised a particular set of questions that I had not given sufficient thought to at the outset of the research. Most notably, although Asian women may share some common experiences of racism with black women of African-Caribbean descent, differences in group location, cultural identity and language distinguish their experiences in specific ways and posed problems for me in accessing these women. In retrospect, I now see that I seriously underestimated the enormity of the task and did not anticipate the formidable obstacles that would be raised in trying to recruit Asian and African women to participate in the study. I came to realise that struggling with these issues brought into sharp focus the complexities involved in attempting to study members of communities that I was not part of. I therefore made the decision to focus my efforts on recruiting black women of African-Caribbean descent. In doing so, I am not claiming "insider status", nor implying that the differences between the respondents and myself would necessarily be lessened (Bernard, 1998). As Back (1996) notes, claiming insider status can result in researchers asserting a privileged right to speak for "the people".

Overall, negotiating access to potential research participants was labour intensive, proved to be extremely frustrating, and did not always result in a beneficial outcome. Johnson (1992) in her study of "Mothers of Incest Survivors" also comments on the difficulties she encountered in trying to locate mothers for her research. A number of other researchers have also made some important points on their attempts to negotiate access with gatekeepers in the process of recruiting research participants. For example, in looking at the experiences of black children in the public care system, Barn (1994) highlights the resistance she encountered from social service departments in her attempts to negotiate access to research participants. In a similar vein, Westcott (1996) noted gatekeepers' reluctance to allow access to potential participants. She suggests that one of the main reasons cited by gatekeepers for being reluctant to allow access to service users is harm or disruption to them. According to Westcott, the reluctance of gatekeepers to allow access to potential research participants is often predicated on fears that, for example, research involving families who were "open cases" would be intrusive to the families and would have an impact on the social work input. Moreover, Westcott found that some service providers contend that research involving "closed cases" may reactivate painful memories for families, thus hindering them "to put their experiences behind them". We are reminded here of Kinard's assertion: "where families have experienced investigation from child protection agencies, they may resent any further intrusion from outside sources" (1994, p. 651). Additionally, it has been noted that research on child sexual abuse is potentially stigmatising to those being researched and families may be reluctant to participate (Lee, 1993). Furthermore, it could convincingly be argued that social work clients, particularly those in institutional care, are increasingly seen as a captive research population by researchers (Mauther, 1997). While I believe wholeheartedly that gatekeepers have the right to question researchers' motives for undertaking research, I nevertheless have difficulty accepting as given that service providers ultimately know what is best for service users concerning decisions about their participation in research projects. I do not doubt that research could be intrusive to families, and indeed, families might even be exploited by the experience without necessarily benefiting from the research. Notwithstanding, it is also possible that for families who are often marginalised and disempowered by the child protection process, sensitively thought-out research could be empowering and strengthening to them by essentially giving them a voice. It is rarely acknowledged that the research experience can be "therapeutic" for participants by providing them with a safe space to give voice to their experiences to a dedicated listener and offers the opportunity to reflect upon their experiences to enhance their current understandings of their situations (King, 1996; Westcott, 1996).

Once I had made contact with suitable mothers who met the study criteria to interview, I had to be assured that they were giving their informed consent to participate in the research. Actualising my good intentions of active participation in the research process required giving careful regard to my research strategies in order to enhance respondents' understanding for them to make an informed decision to participate (King, 1996). I was mindful that some mothers' encounters with the helping professionals might have left them feeling disempowered. Optimally, my intention was to make the research process empowering for the participants, as the informed consent of the mothers was crucial to their effective participation. Perhaps most critically, given that the research raised questions the mothers may have found unsettling and uncomfortable, there were a number of essential factors I had to take into consideration. I was keenly aware that concerns about the use and abuse of research findings might be predominant in some women's minds. To help minimise the respondents' concerns, they were provided with a pre-interview briefing which offered the opportunity for clarification and elaboration about the ideas informing the research and, most importantly, to discuss my motivation for doing the study. Understandably, despite the information provided, some mothers were still ambivalent about taking part in the research and questioned my motives for doing it. Not surprisingly, all the mothers expressed concerns about issues of confidentiality and how the information would be used.

Ethical Concerns

One major area that I had to give consideration to was the issue of confidentiality. King (1996) notes that in the beginning stage of the research, it is necessary to give considerable thought to the potential difficulties and dilemmas that might arise later on. The very nature of this kind of research does definitely mean that certain ethical dilemmas are raised and careful thought was needed about potential areas of conflict at every stage of the research process, most crucially at the point where I was negotiating mothers' consent to be involved in the research. One issue that was essential and inescapable in the context of the research was how I was going to balance the conflicting ethical issues in respect to child protection. Though my research did not involve interviewing the children of the mothers, I nevertheless had to give careful attention to how I might deal with safety issues for children in the context of the research. It was especially important to consider what might happen if a mother revealed information suggesting that her child may still be in a seriously harmful situation. Thus, it was necessary to convey to mothers that where I felt children might be exposed to further harm, if they were unwilling to address their children's safety needs themselves my ethical stance would entail bringing this to the attention of child protection agencies. This would of course mean that I was making judgements about mothers' safety planning and ultimately their understandings of what are safe and unsafe conditions for their children. I therefore had to explore these issues sensitively with mothers, and at the same time avoid taking a judgemental stance against them. Most significantly, I had to explore these issues in order to be clear about how I would manage and resolve any conflict of interest that might ensue. Given the intricacies involved, I was particularly mindful that I needed to be explicit about my ethical stance with the respondents and certainly did not want to give them confused or dishonest messages. Unless I explicitly spelt out my stance, I ran the risk of breaching confidence should the issue arise. However, keeping that in mind helped me to ground the research in an understanding of the safety needs of children. I wanted to hold on to the chief principle of maintaining a clear and critical focus on the safety needs of the children of the research participants. I was guided by an ethical stance that was informed by an awareness of the rights and interests of children and ultimately this meant exploring with the research respondents the limits of confidentiality. Whilst I was acutely aware of the conflicting terrain on which I was negotiating consent, there was little doubt that openness and honesty between the mothers and myself was a vital foundation to mutual understanding. Nevertheless, raising these issues with respondents brought me a sense of unease, and indeed intensified my fears of the inherent risk that I might lose mothers from the sample. However, I was clear that this consideration had to be balanced against the need to remain sensitive to the safety needs of children, whilst at the same time ensuring that the research experience should not be oppressive to mothers.

In this sense, keeping in focus the goals of non-exploitative research, that of respect, openness and clarity of communication, as key features of ethical research practice was of critical importance (Reinharz,

1992). Central to my thinking was that particularly those mothers who had not involved child protection agencies would be fearful that I might report them to child protection services. This, point is relevant, not least because child sexual abuse is largely hidden and there are relative silences around child sexual abuse in black communities, as there is, to some extent, in all communities (Wilson, 1993). Thus, I had to find ways in which to have such discussions with the respondents, but at the same time minimise the likelihood of their withdrawing from the research. Successful recruitment of research participants relied in part on the strength of exploration of these issues with the mothers in order to be clear with them about expectations. Interestingly, raising these issues with the mothers provided me with an avenue for exploring with them one of the key research questions, notably their own perception of risk. The tensions involved in balancing the safety needs of children against the interests of their mothers in the context of the research poses something of a contradiction for researchers. Struggling with these issues brought the realisation that this is an unresolved tension in child abuse research and is an ongoing concern for researchers.

Power in Shaping Consent

My commitment to bringing sensitivity towards studying women's lived experiences necessitated seeking ethical ways to gather data (Kelly, Reagan and Burton, 1994). In particular, 1 had to give careful attention to the way significant power relations might operate on different levels in the research process to disempower respondents. Significantly, I had to consider the way power dynamics might manifest itself to inhibit those respondents who were suggested to me by their social workers from refusing to be part of the research if they did not want to take part. In particular, some may have felt that the service they were receiving from their social workers might be incumbent on them agreeing to be part of the research. The issue of power goes deep in this context not least because some of the mothers may have felt defenseless to say no in the face of powerful professionals. I also had to be mindful that in the aftermath of child sexual abuse, many mothers are rendered with feelings of powerlessness, and the research interview could re-enact such experiences of powerlessness. Feeling disempowered would actively disadvantage women from participating in the research on their own terms and I thus had to be careful not to compound these experiences. Given the importance of these issues, my overriding concern was that the research process did not inadvertently obscure women's experiences of powerlessness and replay or reproduce all the old hierarchies of power relationships (Reinharz, 1992). It was thus critically important that I did not compound women's powerlessness in the process of negotiating access with gatekeepers by any invasive and insensitive research practice and run the risk of reinforcing the very same power relations I was seeking to examine. It was therefore necessary for me to allay respondents' anxieties, for them to feel assured and to see that I was independent from the social services departments. The two-fold irony was that I also had to work extremely hard at maximising cooperation with gatekeepers in order to have access to research participants. Assuring the gatekeepers of my commitment to promoting the safety needs of children was fundamental to my success in accessing mothers who met the criteria. More generally, this last factor was significant for my gaining an "in" to potential participants.

Emotionality in the Research Process

Principally, I wanted to pay maximum attention to the emotional demands of the research on mothers so that I could be attentive to the feelings that arose, in order to alleviate or minimise the stress on the participants. I was mindful that research into child sexual abuse is an emotionally laden field (Schawrtz, 1997), and that discussions about child sexual abuse tend to evoke strong feelings and may indeed make some women hesitant to participate in research. Especially, as the subject matter of child sexual abuse generates strong emotions, I wanted to be sensitive to the impact of my questioning on the research participants. Research on mothers' responses show that they will experience an array of emotions that involve denial, anger, blame, sadness, and despair (Green, 1996; Skinner, 2000). I therefore had to contemplate that for some of the mothers, having to talk about their children's abuse may re-live those emotional conflicts. Consideration of these factors helped me keep in focus the mothers' emotional state to be aware of the feelings and ambivalence that they may bring to the research interview. For example, some mothers might bring a great deal of anxiety and may harbour feelings that I would be judgmental of their responses and the decisions they had taken. Essentially, my thinking was influenced by an understanding of the anxiety engendered in the very nature of the subject matter under study. Most significantly, I needed to pay close attention to the level of stress that the data-gathering might incur for mothers and consider ways to minimise its potentially negative effects. I wanted to use my skills of reflexivity to aid rather than hinder mothers' involvement in the research. In order for the interview to yield important information, it was critical for the mothers to feel able to participate and to be in control of their situation. Overall, my commitment to furthering feminist research principles meant finding ways to ensure that the participants, who were central to the research, were not subjected to an invasive research practice. My concerns throughout have been to create a non-exploitative research experience for the respondents. Kelly, Reagan and Burton's discussion of researching the incidence of violence towards women and children is relevant here. According to these authors, research should aspire "to do no more harm; to endeavour not to exploit; and, where possible, to give something back" (1998, p.606). Thus, finding a balance of enabling the respondents to participate without feeling dissonant from their own experience was of utmost importance.

Pre-interview briefings provided the opportunity for mothers to question me about the research and was not only facilitative to the women for making informed decisions about their participation, but was also a way of dispelling fear and mistrust. Essentially, I saw the sessions as an opportunity to give respondents some choice and control as to whether to take part in the project, and also saw them as another way to optimise respondents' participation. Ultimately, the pre-interview briefings also helped me to clarify that it was ultimately their choice to be part of the research. Additionally, I felt that giving the participants the space to voice their concerns would be another chance for me to reflect on ways that the research experience would not stigmatise or disempower them and gave me further opportunities to deal with questions and areas I may not have given sufficient thought to.

Post-interview debriefs offered the opportunity for respondents to reflect on the processes that took place in the interview and most importantly, to finish the interview and leave behind any "emotional baggage" stirred up by the interview (King, 1996). Specifically, as I did not want respondents to be left feeling exposed and isolated, I made available information of relevant helping agencies and self-help groups where women could seek emotional and practical help for themselves or their children should they require it. The very nature of the subject matter of the research means there is a danger that the role of the researcher can become blurred. There may be the potential to be drawn into a counselling or advice-giving role, thus making it difficult to maintain an intellectual distance (Hammersley and Atkinson, 1995; Skinner, 1998). Providing information about help-giving agencies to respondents was one way of offering support, but it also helped me to establish boundaries and clarity around the nature of the interviews. It also offered an avenue for those respondents who had not previously sought help outside of their immediate families to deal with the aftermath of the abuse. Moreover, it helped me to pursue a key goal in feminist research, that of reciprocity in the research process (Reinharz, 1992).

Data Gathering and Analysis

A grounded theory approach was used as a framework for the data gathering and analysis (Glaser and Strauss, 1967). Because a central goal of the research is to generate theory from the data to construct new knowledge of the multiplicity of black mothers' experiences, a grounded theory approach was considered the most relevant analytical tool to analyse mothers' accounts. Grounded theory is a qualitative research approach that offers a framework for inductively building theory through the qualitative analysis of data (Strauss and Corbin, 1990). The underlying assumption of a grounded theory approach is essentially that of formulating theoretical interpretations of data grounded in lived experiences. The advantage of a grounded theory approach for this study is that it offers a framework to analyse experiences that are infused with multiple and often complex interpretations and meanings (Pidgeon and Henwood, 1996). But especially, as there is an under-theorising of black mothers' perspectives of child sexual abuse in the literature, a grounded-theory approach had much to offer as a method for elucidating theoretical perspectives directly from the data (Taylor and Bogdan, 1984).

In-depth semi-structured interviews covering a number of broad themes were conducted with the mothers as a data collecting technique. Open-ended questions were used as a method of data-gathering and my questions were framed in a non-blaming and supportive manner. In seeking to understand the complexities of black mothers' situations, I wanted a framework that enabled mothers to express their underlying attitudes and to discuss the issues of particular concern to them from a frame of reference that reflected their experiences. In this sense, I drew on the thinking of qualitative researchers who advocate that a qualitative approach can better uncover and understand what lies behind a

31

phenomenon that is little explored (Strauss and Corbin, 1990). However, a critique of open-ended questions is that they leave the interpretation of the response to the researcher. As Reay (1996) contends, issues of reflexivity, power and truth impact on the interpretation of the data in very complex ways. The interviews ranged in duration from one to two hours (averaging one and a half-hours in length) and were tape-recorded. All the participants were given an "opt out" clause stating that they were not compelled to answer all the questions, and that they could stop the interview at any time (King, 1996). I conducted all the interviews myself, but utilised the help of a research assistant to transcribe the interviews. Once transcribed, all identifying information was deleted from the transcript and stored confidentially and the interviews were identifiable by a coding system known only to myself.

In keeping with the grounded theory approach, the data-gathering and analysis took place simultaneously through the data collection phase. The interview transcripts generated data grouped around a number of categories on the effects of child sexual abuse, mothers' reactions to the disclosure/discovery, support services received and mothers' constructions of risk. Each interview was subsequently analysed using these categories (Kelly, Reagan and Burton, 1998). According to grounded theorists, reflecting the constant processes theoretical sampling, constant comparison and the use of coding paradigms facilitate the generation of conceptual development (Glaser and Strauss, 1967; Strauss, 1987; Strauss and Corbin, 1990; Pidgeon and Henwood, 1996). For example, very early in the data-gathering phase, by making constant comparisons, the concept of divided loyalty was employed as a conceptual framework for analysing the conflictual terrain of mothers' experiences (the analytical category divided loyalty was developed from the data and is explored in greater detail in chapter four).

Limitations of the Study

There are some possible limitations to this research. Most notably, any criticism levelled at this study may centre on questions of validity, reliability and generalisability (Ribbens and Edwards, 1998; Hammersley, 1996). In particular, it lays the research open to the charge that because the mothers are self-selected the sample is biased. I suspect that those mothers who may have found it difficult to believe and support their children might not have been willing to take part in the research. A complicated factor is that there are difficulties in collecting retrospective information. Clearly, as the mothers in this study are providing a retrospective account, it is a possibility that some mothers' accounts may be distorted. It is certainly possible that mothers' versions of reality may not reflect the "truth" (Strauss and Corbin, 1990), as experience is remembered selectively (Hester, Pearson and Harwin, 1998). Most notably, mothers' accounts may be coloured by their hindsight (Renzetti, 1997). It is worth noting that personal and collective survival is based on the repression of the memory of past events that are too painful (Pajaczkowska and Young, 1992). Moreover, it is quite conceivable that in telling their version of events, some mothers may be selective in what they remember, or indeed give socially desirable responses to the questions by responding in a way they think is more acceptable to the researcher. Therefore, there may be omissions in some mothers' accounts, whilst some may recount their versions of events in such a way as to enhance themselves to appear in a more positive light. In essence, what are missing from these accounts are the viewpoints of the children as to what constitutes a supportive response from their mothers. Another dimension that is missing from this research is the perspective of the professional helpers where they were involved. In short, it is very likely that we would get a different picture had the study included the perspectives of their children or professional helpers. However, this was not the focus of the study; fundamentally, the study set out to understand mothers' feelings and experiences of the abuse of their children from their specific perspective.

Another criticism that could be levelled is that the study sample is small and the mothers interviewed will not necessarily represent all black mothers. One such consequence of this concern is that the work would be dismissed as being partial. The research does not claim to be a comprehensive account of black mothers' experiences. Nor do I assume grand assertions about monolithic ideas of black mothers. Clearly, no one piece of research is likely to address the factors facing all black mothers of abused children. Ultimately, black mothers are multi-voiced and will not necessarily have a shared understanding of the experience of being a black mother of an abused child. Though black women may have some shared experiences (such as racism, discrimination, or a shared history of migration), they are differentiated around lines of class, ethnicity, cultural background, and education; ultimately, their personal biographies will powerfully shape the multiple dimensions of their responses in the aftermath of child sexual abuse. So naturally, these findings cannot be generalised to all black mothers, and results of a small-scale study such as this is more illuminative rather than conclusive. In spite of these limitations the advantage of the research is that it explores new territories and will be of value for the insights it provide for unravelling the complex and multi-faceted ways race, and gender intersect to shape mothers' responses to the sexual abuse of their children. This perspective has to be an important starting point.

4 Divided Loyalty: Mothers' Emotional and Behavioural Responses to the Abuse of their Children

> Talking about the experience has raised some questions for me that I thought I had dealt with. However, I knew it would be a beneficial experience for me to talk about it. That's why I did it.
> *Mother of a child that had been abused*

This chapter describes mothers' emotional and behavioural responses in the aftermath of the abuse of their children to unravel the multiple determining factors that influenced such responses. Drawing on the findings of the study, the paradigm of divided loyalty is employed as a conceptual framework for analysing important facets of the emotional experiences of mothers. It is argued that to appreciate the feelings evoked for mothers in the aftermath of abuse, conceptually understanding divided loyalty as a key component in mothers' emotions provides important glimpses into the contradictions and ambiguities embodied in their emotion.

Divided Loyalty

In order to make sense of mothers' emotional responses, the overriding question that needs to be asked is what does discovery mean for this group of mothers? To begin to answer this question, a starting point has to be an appreciation that the discovery of abuse was a painful and very difficult time for all the mothers involved. The accounts of mothers in this study indicate that the effects of their children's abuse stirred up powerful emotions that provoked conflictual loyalties. The range of emotions and feelings that mothers were faced with encompassed anxiety, depression, disassociation, disbelief, shame, silence, sadness, and guilt. Indeed, what seemed to most characterise these mothers' emotional reactions were themes of conflict, powerlessness, uncertainty and perhaps importantly, feeling a deep sense of anger and betrayal. Studies highlight that denial, anger, and disbelief, are stages that are seen in mothers' reactions as they go through what can only be likened to the bereavement process (Hooper, 1992; Johnson, 1992; Skinner, 2000; Sgroi and Dana, 1982). It has been noted that mothers may swing between belief, disbelief and avoidance and may go through a process of denial, depression and finally acceptance of the inevitability of the situation (Green, 1996). To begin with disclosure, or crucially, how mothers come to find out about the abuse, is a complex process involving a number of dynamics. It is important to keep in mind that there is a continuum of disclosure, which means that it should be seen as a process involving a number of influencing dynamics (Smith, 1995). These dynamics include not only mothers' emotional states, but also their relationships with their children, and wider family networks, and most critically if he is the abuser, their relationship with their partners. An important point to stress here is that the stages that mothers go through should not be seen in isolation but should be evaluated in the context of their everyday lived realities. Sexual abuse is a shattering and acutely painful experience, first and foremost for the child involved, but it causes pain and destruction to all family members, and family functioning is affected in the most profound way. Clearly, intrafamilial abuse strikes at the very heart of family relationships, and most powerfully, norms and beliefs are destabilised. For mothers, the discovery of intrafamilial abuse is especially painful and disruptive particularly because it evokes powerful and uncomfortable feelings and sets into action a train of events that bring family members to crisis point. More often than not, loyalties, attachments, and lines of allegiance are all thrown into question and family members are presented with a challenge to re-evaluate their relationships with each other. It is from this frame of conflict and contradictions that mothers have to disentangle the different strands of feelings and emotions to respond to their children's needs following abuse.

It is very likely that the emotions evoked in the aftermath of abuse may be similar for all mothers regardless of their race however, the point of departure for black mothers is that the nexus of race and gender relationships, means there are some specific ways their emotional responses are influenced by the intersecting effects of these dimensions. Faced with the devastating consequences of the abuse, a number of mothers in the study talked of the emotional turmoil for them in having to balance a range of conflictual allegiances. Essentially, the impact of abuse makes black mothers' needs and preoccupations distinctly different to other groups of mothers. Therefore, although it can be argued that the notion of divided loyalty is a powerful dimension in the reality for most mothers on the discovery of intrafamilial sexual abuse, inevitably, black mothers' concerns would undoubtedly be affect by the institutional racism that structures their lives; notably in how this factor would influence their perceptions of the options they felt they had open to them.

It is necessary to reflect on the interacting factors that influence how mothers come to make sense of their children's abuse. Though there were many similarities in the mothers' emotional responses, a noteworthy difference was whether the abuse was intrafamilial or extrafamilial. Especially when abuse is intrafamilial and the abuser was the children's father, a striking consistent feature throughout the mothers' accounts were the ways in which they all experienced a range of mixed feelings of loyalty to men that conflicted with their allegiance to their children. It has been argued elsewhere that especially where the abuser is the father, it placed mother and child in positions of mutual betrayal (Miller, 1990).

This mother's account illustrates some of the ways painful betrayal is felt:

> My immediate reactions were feelings of shame and betrayal. I felt very hurt and betrayed for my daughter. The thing that made it worse was that I knew that behind my back, family and friends were saying I was letting my husband sleep with my girl child – as if I knew about it and did nothing. It felt as if I had to suffer the shame alone and in silence. And what made it worse was that it was me that was left to pick up the pieces and help my daughter make sense of her relationship with her father after what he had subjected her to.

A key issue for this mother was how she coped with the painful reality of her child's abuse and made sense of her relationship with her husband. This mother felt the sense of betrayal most acutely. Here we can see how this mother seemed to be struggling intensely with painful contradictions of loyalty and deep-rooted emotional conflicts that led to personal dilemmas.

The findings of this research indicate that where the children's fathers were the alleged abuser these mothers tended on the whole, not to have been the ones who initiated reporting the abuse outside the home; the abuse may have come to light through children's behaviour coming to the

37

attention of teachers or other authority figures, or the child disclosing to someone outside the home. These findings are consistent with what has been found in other research, notably, that intrafamilial sexual abuse, particularly father-daughter abuse, is less likely to be reported outside the home (Russell, 1986).

Considering the saliency of the meanings black mothers bring to bear on their relationship with their partners in the aftermath of abuse, a number of issues are intertwined. It would appear that one area of tension for the mothers involves the complexities embodied in their relationship with the men in their lives. The reasons for this are multi-faceted but at the heart of this tension is the need to understand something of the complex way racism shapes the nature of black women's emotional and psychological relatedness and connectedness to black men. Part of the complexity for black women has to do with the fact that because of living with the daily reality of racism there may be unique empathic ties between black women and men. Robinson and Ward (1991) alert us to the idea that black women must resist an individualism that sees the self as disconnected from others in the black community. Moreover, it is suggested that when you add gender socialisation processes into this equation you have a complex relational nexus that imbues in black women the need to facilitate bonds with black men, sometimes at the expense of their own needs (Hill Collins, 1990). As has been highlighted most succinctly: "The socialisation process is also responsible for determining two seemingly incompatible facts: (1) the Black woman defining herself, and her existence in relation to Black men; (2) while simultaneously seeing herself as an independent being" (Dodson, quoted in Joseph, 1991, p. 94). This set of dynamics introduces a layer of complexity for black women in terms of how they come to see themselves as separate but also as part of an interconnected web in their relationships with black men (Bryan, Dadzie and Scafe 1985). Fundamentally for black women, the construction of the black female self emerges through complex processes of racial and gendered contradictions. Thus, a key factor framing mothers' relationships with black men is that they are painfully aware of the ways racist imagery demonises black males and promotes a negative stereotyping of black males' sexuality that depicts them as uncontrollable, amoral, and licentious (Marshall, 1994; Smith, 1998). The lasting effects of the negative representation is that an image of black males is proffered as the dangerous "other" thus perpetuating the myth of the hypersexual black male (Mercer and Julien, 1988). A case in point is that when a black man is accused of rape or abuse, racist stereotyping will attribute the problem to black culture (Droisen, 1989); whereas if a white man is accused of rape, or other forms of sexual violence it is seldom constructed as a problem afflicting the whole white race but would be put down to individual pathology (Smith, 1998). Not surprisingly, therefore mothers experience a range of feelings and are presented with conflicts that pose fundamental challenges for making immediate decisions about their relationships to abusive men, in which the safety needs of their children are paramount. The tension for mothers essentially, is that when sexual abuse is discovered it presents them with a contradictory set of feelings of loyalty to partners mixed with anger and betrayal. Many factors converge to mean that in their efforts to make sense of the abuse mothers' wrestle with feelings of collective responsibility towards black men that generate conflictual emotions. So even on the discovery of sexual abuse, black women who are acutely aware of societal perceptions of black men may find it difficult to envisage child protection agencies as the holders of solutions to the problem on resolving violence and abuse in black families. Unquestionably, the discovery of abuse is a major factor in challenging mothers to rethink their lives. Their perception of their emotional weddedness to black men means that mothers were forced in one way or another to confront questions of self, subjectivity and identity. It essentially means mothers have to construct new meanings into their relationship with their partners at a time when they are experiencing acute uncertainties.

This is how one mother of a ten-year-old girl who was abused by her husband described her feelings:

> I knew I was using avoidance and withdrawal as a way of dealing with what had happened to my daughter. I was feeling empty and hurt and experiencing numbness. At the time I couldn't think rationally about any other way to deal with the situation. I was struggling on my own with little support from anyone and it was very hard to know what my true feelings were.

The tensions and dilemmas for black mothers are further compounded when we also take into account their relationship with their wider kinship support networks. The main significance of women's wider kinship network is twofold: first, in the way some mothers felt some accountability towards family and community; second, in the extent to which the notion of family and community remain inextricably linked to how some of the women saw their identities as mothers. A layer of

39

complexity for these mothers is that in the context of a racist society where black people are subject to a constant barrage of external negative valuations, the family is a sanctuary from the daily defence against racism. Consequently, the place of home and family is of salience to black women, men and children who are devalued by a large part of British society; their families may be the only safe space they have against racism. Black mothers are all too mindful of Eurocentric conceptualisation of black families within a problem-oriented paradigm. It is usually to their families that many black women turn to for affirmation of self and a source of validation. However, in the event of abuse coming to light, in essence, mothers have to confront their own illusory notions of the family as being a safe space for all its members. Clearly the reality does not live up to the expectations for their children. The realisation for some of these mothers was that they were left emotionally unsupported, and perhaps, most critically, the normative assumptions that the home is a safe haven for them and their children from a racist world are unsettled. Wounded in the place you should know love represents a terrible betrayal especially for the children involved, but also for their mothers (hooks, 2000).

Mothers reported that they had to reconcile a number of tensions in order to make the right choices that promoted the well being of their children. Conceivably, a key question that is raised is whether extended family members may experience black mothers' help seeking outside their families as acts of betrayal. What most distressed a number of mothers were the family members who interpreted their reporting the abuse outside the family as betraying their race. In fact mothers' requests for support were often met with a resounding silence. And yet, while mothers invariably viewed their children's abuse as a form of betrayal, ironically, families saw mothers' reporting of the abuse to child protection agencies as a form of betrayal. A number of mothers spoke of coming under intense pressure from other family members to keep quiet about the abuse. Thus, these mothers, who were quite rightly striving to promote the interests of their children, were successfully cast in the 'black women as traitor of the race' role (Hill Collins, 1998). What some mothers found out to their cost is that breaking the silence and talking about the abuse outside the home is risky and carries repercussions. At stake is their membership in their families and communities. Some of the difficulties that have given rise are that some mothers experienced a distance from their families in the aftermath of the abuse, which exacerbated feelings of isolation. With little emotional stamina mothers reported feeling very fragile and often succumbed to family pressure. The most crucial factor that contributed to the decision-making of those mothers who did not report the abuse to anyone outside the home was pressure from partners and families coupled with their own guilt, confused feelings and most importantly fear of other people's reactions. It is important to consider the way that extended family support networks can overtly and covertly exert a powerful influence on mothers not to involve the helping agencies that are there to assist with the protection of children.

Here one mother describes the response she received when she told her sister about the allegations her eight-year-old daughter had made against her sister's husband:

> Why are you telling me this now, why are you trying to create problems in my relationship was what she kept saying. She seemed mostly concerned that I did not talk to anyone else about it, especially other family members. Whereas I felt I wanted to warn other family members with girl children to be careful about leaving them unsupervised around her husband, she wanted me to just keep quiet.

In situations of sexual abuse we need to explode the myth that the family is always there to help and give support in times of crisis. What is evident from this example is that this mother was looking for support in a family made tenuous by the abuse and riven with contradictions. It may well be that the attitudes of mothers' families may be an important influence on their emotional reactions. Thus, mothers' network of support of family and friends may be limited, leaving them susceptible to isolation and depression. Mothers were in effect struggling to hold two contradictory positions: to extol the virtues of the family as harmonious and conflict free, whilst at the same time striving to give their children emotional support by indications of their unconditional loyalty. One might ask how the meaning of social ties reinforced prevailing gendered assumptions about women's loyalty thus posing the dilemmas that underscored these mothers' emotional responses. This point is worthy of consideration because the meaning of social ties exerted a strong influence and shaped expectations about obligations and responsibilities that ostensibly put the burden on women to be silent. Women's voices are silenced through processes of power and control and a number equated their situations to a state of being psychologically paralysed. To be sure, the pressures resulted in some mothers feeling coerced into conspiring in the silence about male abuses in the home. The problem here lies in the tension between family expectations and mothers' wants and feelings. Commentators hooks (1995) and Hill Collins (1998) have been prompted to remark on the pressures exerted by black family support systems on black women to conform to certain gendered expectations around loyalty. Accordingly, Hill Collins (1998) noted that within some black families, there is a taken-for-grantedness, almost an unwritten rule, that black women will support black men no matter what has happened. Similarly, hooks (1995) contends that efforts on the part of black women to assert their agency over their lives is perceived as attacks on black manhood and acts of betrayal. On the contrary, hooks, cogently argues: "black females must not allow ourselves to be duped into supporting shit that hurts us under the guise of standing beside our men" (hooks, 1994, p.123).

Thus, the family as a site where black mothers everyday lived realities may be experienced as oppressive may remain unchallenged. Familial relationships can affirm traditional gender roles, consequently veiling power relationships and ultimately leaves unquestioned assumptions about women's undivided loyalty to men. It becomes apparent that racialised and gendered power relations interplay in contradictory ways for the mothers so that they occupy a number of positions of loyalty that created inherent tensions for them in giving voice to their children's experience of sexual abuse. Identifying how race and gender relations shape black mothers relationships in their families will open up important glimpses into their circumstances and help pinpoint the situations that may undermine their ability to give the right kind of support to their children in the aftermath of abuse. In essence, analysis of the factors shaping mothers' lived experiences can deepen understandings of the cultural and social processes that they have to negotiate in order for them to make the right choices to meet the needs of their children.

Anger and Ambivalence

Undoubtedly, with the discovery of sexual abuse, the emotional impact on mothers was to fuel an intense rage and anger that sometimes manifested itself in a very self-destructive way. Indeed, in their struggles to deal with their own conflicting emotions some mothers internalised or displaced their anger onto themselves.

This is painfully illustrated by this mother's reflections:

The anger is still around so I'm very dismissive of people because it is difficult to trust. I know I'm over-eating and smoking too much as a way of dealing with my feelings. I'm feeling a lot of pain.

When people are too traumatised to speak about painful experiences they can internalise their anger. Almost invariably, a number of mothers expressed anger at themselves for not picking up sooner that something was going on.

This mother whose ten-year-old daughter was abused by her husband provides an example to illustrate this point:

I felt as if I was swallowing my anger. You begin to feel paranoid. As if everyone is thinking you should have noticed something. I feel afraid to trust anyone.

One mother whose six-year-old daughter was abused by her stepfather, (the mothers' husband) remarks:

I am either feeling very angry or withdrawn. I don't know whom to trust anymore. I was even afraid to acknowledge the abuse to myself so it feels easier to shut myself off from everyone. I'm more fearful and I feel as if I have to become a different person.

In the face of multifarious obstacles and debilitating contradictions, perhaps not surprisingly some mothers' emotional responses were not devoid of ambivalence. Even though some mothers had a lot of anger towards their husbands or partners, the fact remained that they continued to have mixed feelings towards them. Significantly, a number of mothers had somewhat ambivalent feelings towards their partners, which ultimately created blocks to acting decisively. Some even continued an ambivalent relationship with their partners with devastating consequences for their relationship with their children.

Here one mother recounts some of her ambivalent feelings:

I was in a difficult and shameful situation. I did not leave the marriage immediately and that to me makes it more shameful. I felt guilty as if I was to blame for what had happened to my daughter. I kept thinking if I was a better wife, you know, all that kind of thing was going through my mind and if I am honest with myself I was frightened of loosing my husband. I did not tell my family or anyone else what was going on. At the time I thought I was dealing with things, but in looking back, I was in

43

a fog, I was like in denial, and that was probably the worst thing to do for the difficulties it created in my relationship with my daughter. The marriage eventually broke down about two years later when I plucked up the courage to stop living a lie.

The fact that this mother had confused emotions about her partner contributed to her ambivalent feelings. Loyalty played a pivotal role in sustaining that ambivalence. It is precisely the nature of the ambivalent feelings that served to exacerbate this mother's feelings of guilt and being torn in several directions, because she was acutely aware of the emotional fall-out her choices would bring and therefore had to weigh up the consequences and the actions that flows from it. This mother clearly needed space to work through her ambivalent feelings to understand the conflict in her emotional responses to the abuse and the implications for her relationship with her daughter.

Accordingly, ambivalence also constrained some mothers from accessing appropriate help and support. The mother of a twelve-year-old girl who was abused by her husband, the child's father, had this to say:

> Talking about an experience which was black on black with white professionals was very difficult to do. I kept thinking they must have been thinking this is typical of black families. It felt that as if something like that is happening in your family is maybe a justification for how the white society sees you in the first place.

As this account illustrates, a number of important dimensions underlie mothers' emotional responses. Most notably, the fear of racism was an important inhibitor to some of the mothers speaking of the abuse outside the family. Such emotions may also signify mothers' particular concerns that negative perceptions of black families will inform interpretations of the abuse. Ultimately, however, the critical role gendered power relations played in evoking secrecy and silence and contribute to mothers' ambivalent feelings cannot be underestimated. Mothers are effectively in a double-bind situation, which creates ambivalent feelings and fuels secrecy about sexual abuse.

A mother whose ten-year-old daughter was abused by her partner provides another example that illustrates how racism contributes to ambivalent feelings:

There was a pressure – not only from white society, but within your own society, like a lot of covering up. The pressure is there to cover up.

It is this conflict that is at the root of some mothers' ambivalence. The ambivalence that configures mothers' emotional responses derives essentially from the intersecting effects of race and gender oppression in operation in their lives. Most specifically, race and gender intersected to create powerful and conflicting feelings of loyalty that are difficult to reconcile. This in turn fuelled ambivalence that acted to powerfully immobilise a number of the mothers; ultimately, hindering them from giving full voice to their children's experiences of abuse in the home. Therefore, what may appear as collusive silence on issues of child sexual abuse could be interpreted as one of the consequences of ambivalent feelings. However, an important point to keep in mind is that maintaining the silence effectively got in the way of these mothers' abilities to explore their emotional reactions thus disenabling some from being a source of support to their children. Clearly, some mothers' ambivalence, it seemed, prevented them from having insight into the effects of the abuse on their children. Whilst silence may be a strategic response to a position of powerlessness, child protection professionals could easily interpret mothers' silence as either tacit acceptance or active complicity. Furthermore, one can posit that children might interpret their mother's silence as consent. Insofar as silence need not mean consent then it might be relevant to consider that some mothers may be in denial about what had happened to their children. Another point to emphasise here is that in making judgements about mothers' silence, the complex power relationships that underscore their emotions can easily be ignored. Recognising the complexities in mothers' emotional reactions opens up our thinking to the way strong loyalties developed in the context of how racism may foster ambivalence in mothers. The important insight here is that a number of contradictions, tensions and dilemmas are raised for mothers that means their responses do not fit comfortably within the collusion paradigm. It may well be that mothers' uncertainties and ambivalences need to be understood in the context of powerlessness rather than within the collusion paradigm.

Cognitive Dissonance

Given the picture of contradictions, conflictual allegiances and ambivalence that abound, perhaps not surprisingly, the majority of the mothers experienced some form of cognitive dissonance. In how mothers described their emotional responses, what emerged clearly was the dissonance between what some believed and the reality of what they felt and did (Joyce, 1999). Mothers reported knowing something was not quite right, and that intuition told them they needed to do something but it was as if their minds would not allow them to believe what they knew to be true. On the one hand these mothers were certain of what they needed to do to protect their children from further risk. On the other hand their feelings were sometimes at odds with their intuitive inclination. Several mothers described feeling as if they were going mad and to have voiced their feelings would have meant speaking the unspeakable: that their partners really are capable of abusing their children.

As this example of a mother whose nine-year-old daughter was abused by her stepfather illustrates:

> I knew I needed to do something to help my daughter but it was as if I was in shock. I could not believe that this had happened to her. I kept running it over and over in my mind asking myself why. When I plucked up the courage to confront my husband, he insisted that she was lying. I spent days, weeks it seems, swinging between belief and disbelief. However, I knew deep down that she was telling the truth but it was as if I did not want to believe that it was true, that my daughter had been abused.

The relationship between thought and behaviour can be complex, and for some mothers their actions were dissonant with their feelings and thinking. In short, the intricate cognitive processes that underlie mothers' feelings meant that their thoughts and behaviours often did not mesh. In a situation of so much conflictual feelings mothers did not trust what they feel and doubt sapped their strength and powerfully immobilised them from acting immediately. The important insight here is that mothers therefore may not know how to act in the face of uncertainty.

By contrast, the mother of a six-year-old girl who was abused by her stepfather had this to say:

The whole process is very tiring, it's very time and life consuming. It can alter your self-esteem...your directions in life. I was extremely confused - feeling angry, feeling inadequate, feeling stupid.

In thinking about the cognitive dissonance embodied in mothers' emotional responses it is important to be aware of the many factors that interplay for black mothers. There is a sense in which the conflicting feelings of loyalty adversely affected mothers by creating additional stressors that have a bearing on their psychological functioning. The inherent contradiction for mothers not only increased their anxieties but also compounded feelings of shame and stigma, and we may speculate as to whether it contributed to some women's depression, isolation and feelings of hopelessness. Some became mired in their own doubts and questioned why they did not notice anything sooner.

Here, the mother of a twelve-year-old girl, who disclosed to a teacher at school that her boyfriend was abusing her daughter, offered these reflections:

I feel stupid because it happened and I hadn't picked up the signs of it. It started appearing in my head, why didn't you tell me, why didn't you tell me, why didn't I know? I have been wanting to know what happened, and the right thing to do, and feeling very stupid.

Reflecting on their reactions, some mothers indicated that on finding out about the abuse they were influenced by the thinking that they were to blame, and that they were failed mothers. For some, confused emotions meshed with unexamined beliefs that they had to remain silent to protect their race all contributed to their feelings of uncertainty. Thus, some felt ashamed and guilty that they were unable to acknowledge immediately that there was a major problem. Let us consider that in order to make sense of their children's abuse, mothers need to be able to give voice to their thoughts and feelings. However, to be able to give voice to their feelings, these mothers have to make sense of a set of mutually related processes; the specificity of the power relations embodied in their families and the very real and concrete ways race and gender dynamics are central to those relationships. That a number of mothers did not have the space to explore their conflict-ridden feelings meant that they were not immediately in touch with their emotions. It is especially important to understand that these complex and intricate processes impact on mothers' adaptive functioning and significantly influenced their capacity to assert their

47

agency and informed the way in which they accessed outside help. Understanding how the simultaneous effects of race and gender oppression operate to shape how mothers may experience cognitive dissonance is important for helping us to make sense of their adaptive functioning.

There are further layers of complexities for mothers in making sense of the cognitive dissonance they experienced. It is necessary to appreciate how the dissonance involved in continually having your experiences as black women marginalised or rendered invisible can have a silencing effect (Burstow, 1992). Silence and invisibility are the hallmarks of black mothers' daily experiences and these augment feelings of discord. It is by bringing to bear an appreciation of the contradictory processes that lie at the heart of mothers' experiences, that we can begin to make the connections between the way mothers think and act in order to unravel the individual circumstances for interpreting their motivations and behaviours in the aftermath of abuse. Clearly, an analysis that is sensitive to mothers' adaptive processes can provide insights into the defence mechanisms in operation for mothers in order to make the links between thought and behaviour.

The "Strong Black Woman" Image

Paradoxically, mothers felt they had to present themselves as strong and coping. A noteworthy finding is that a constraining factor on mothers' abilities to seek emotional and practical support was internalisation of the "strong black woman" image. To appreciate the impact of this notion on mothers' emotional responses it is important to understand the way prevailing cultural portrayals of black womanhood represent black women as emotionally strong, dominant and able to withstand any challenge life throws at them (Mama, 1995; Villorasa, 1994; West, 1999). Most significantly, internalisation of this notion can affect belief systems and exert a controlling influence on mothers to present themselves as psychologically and emotionally strong. The reality is of course far more complex for unconsciously, the "strong black woman" image induced a self-imposed silence, which effectively inhibited some mothers from acknowledging and talking openly about their emotional responses to the abuse of their children. It needs to be emphasised very strongly that a number of the mothers in the study were in fact isolated, confused, deeply hurt and with little outlet to express their true feelings and emotions.

48

Essentially, some mothers ignored or dismissed their hurt and pain as a sign of weakness, ostensibly minimising the significance of their reactions. This state of affairs increased the likelihood of mothers experiencing additional emotional turmoil that compounded feelings of shame, stigma and guilt and ultimately meant increased feelings of diminished self-worth, but particularly sealed mothers' isolation. As such, they were constrained in thinking through the emotional and psychological consequences of the abuse for their children. The belief that women could take care of themselves was pervasive and particularly restricted some mothers' opportunities for seeking emotional and practical support from others. Indeed, the dominant influence of the "strong black woman" image operated to mask deep anxieties about expressing vulnerabilities and in the process isolated many of the mothers thus effectively misrepresenting their lived realities (Mama, 1995).

This mother describes her feelings:

> On discovering that my daughter had been abused by her father I had no one to talk to. It dawned on me that it was always me that everyone turned to when there was a problem to sort out. I suppose I was primarily the nurturer and provider of emotional support to family and friends. I felt I had no one to turn to for help at a time when I most needed support, advice and care. I therefore had to rely on my own emotional resources to help my child come to terms with sexual abuse. At the same time, I had to conceal from my family my hurt and pain and the difficulties I was experiencing. It was a very stressful time.

This example presents vividly some of the tensions that arise for mothers. What is illuminated most clearly is that mothers are grappling with embedded contradictions and ambiguities. And yet, when we consider the conflicting feelings and powerlessness mothers were struggling with, the irony of the "strong black woman" image emerged as a paradox for the majority of mothers. Ultimately, not only did the abuse remain unspoken about, but also some mothers felt immobilised and faced an uphill struggle to assert their strength just when it is most needed to act decisively. This situation has major implications not only for mothers' own psychological health, but also for children's long-term emotional needs. One obvious consequence for children is that their mothers silence effectively blocked their rights to have their needs met. A major consequence is that the children of these mothers may not be encouraged to express their emotional traumas in the aftermath of abuse in order to aid the healing processes. What is more, mothers may consciously or unconsciously be passing on messages to their abused daughters that they should be strong and "get on with it" (Few, 1999; Wyatt, 1997). In terms of the mothers, there are potential psychological consequences, such as depression. Research tells us that mothers who are depressed are hindered in their abilities to be emotionally available to their children (Trowell and Bower, 1995).

In drawing attention to the contradictions embedded in the "strong black woman" image, it is not my intention to inscribe a paradigm of victimisation to represent black mothers as passive and lacking in any agency. Rather, I am interested in showing how the inscription in the psyche of the image of the "strong black woman" has a significant psychological impact and presented barriers for some mothers to be in touch with the emotional impact of their children's abuse on themselves in order to effectively address their children's needs in the aftermath of abuse. Underlying this argument is the belief that particularly on issues such as child sexual abuse that are shameful to reveal, the internalisation of the "strong black woman" image, coupled with the uncertainties generated by conflicting loyalties can create a recipe for denial, silence and distortion. Clearly, it is difficult to assert that black women always internalise this notion unproblematically. Indeed, it is also the case that women will bring their individual resilience mechanism and thus would vary in their internalisation of this notion. Though the view of the "strong black woman" may be a stereotype, nevertheless its influence is real and pervasive and women will doubtless internalise some of these ideas, which would shape their coping mechanisms. Essentially, calling attention to these dynamics illuminates the dilemmas facing mothers and highlights most powerfully that they were coping with multiple layers of complexities which structure their emotional responses. By examining the "strong black woman" imagery it becomes possible to pinpoint the way mothers may devalue and minimise their feelings ultimately masking their emotional reactions. What is important to understand is that the "strong black woman" image can operate to distort the everyday realities of black women's experiences within the family by masking power relations (Villorasa, 1994). Thus, mothers may not be conscious of the underlying feelings that are fuelling their emotions to be in touch with their emotional responses to their children.

Discussion

In exploring the emotional reactions of mothers to the sexual abuse of their children, what has been identified and analysed throughout this chapter are the multiple implications of divided loyalties. Above all, the usefulness of charting the trajectory of mothers' emotional reactions is that it provides important insights into the ambiguities and uncertainties that are deeply embedded in their responses. The role of loyalty feelings in creating conflictual emotions for mothers has to be illuminated to show how these factors shape events and meanings. In essence, this chapter has sought to show that a different conception of black mothers' emotional reactions is necessary and needs to be firmly rooted in the context of their lived realities and everyday experiences to make explicit the complex interrelationships between race, gender and power dynamics in framing their emotions. Arguably, calling attention to the intricate intersecting factors in black mothers' lives will illuminate the subtleties in the way male power and authority in the home, in the guise of a concern for family and community loyalty, is used to subordinate women's and children's needs in their families. Notably, an examination of the interwoveness and interconnectedness of gender and race in effect makes visible the masked power relationships that are at the heart of black mothers' relationships and underscore divided loyalty. Power threads through mothers' experiences in a number of significant ways and its most tangible expression is in the way it imbues behaviour and enforces strict codes for them to conform to ultimately create emotional dilemmas around the notion of loyalty. Most significantly, power relations operated to silence the voices of mothers. Essentially, situating mothers' emotional experiences within the broader context of their lived realities will elucidate that mothers responses are characterised by a number of contradictions they have to negotiate in their lives. As they grapple to construct meanings and understandings to their children's victimisation, they also have to wrestle with a number of conflicts in their attempts to help them come to terms with the debilitating effects of child sexual abuse.

Given the complexities involved for mothers, it is a necessary critical task for helping professionals to question, acknowledge and confront mothers' lived realities in order to not only make sense of their behaviour and motivations, but most importantly, to understand the connections between emotions and behaviour (Williams, 1999). Equally, it is important to consider that judgements will have to be made as to whether mothers' emotional state will affect their ability to offer appropriate care and protection to their children. In balancing the competing needs and demands between mothers and their children, an approach that is underpinned with an understanding of the constraining factors on mothers will be better able to recognise the challenges posed for them in promoting the welfare needs of their children. It is by grasping the complexities that the factors in mothers' lives that positively or negatively impact on their emotional capacity to respond in a protective way to their children can be identified. Ultimately, delineating multifaceted strands of influence will be critical for making evaluative judgements about the risks attached to specific behaviours. As highlighted, a major tension in the believing process for mothers involves their struggles with loyalty. The presumption that mothers should be able to act immediately to protect their children predominates thinking and these ideas may inform professionals' interventions with mothers. It is especially relevant for professional helpers to be aware of the variety of factors that constrain mothers' choices, as it is possible that black mothers' attempts to manage the dilemmas in their lives could be construed as disavowing all responsibilities for their actions. In some ways, of course, it may be all too easy to conclude that mothers' behaviours and the choices that they make are complicitous. Although this is a useful point of reference, important to keep in mind is that this notion is predicated on the assumption that mothers must be cognisant with the effects of the abuse on their children. The collusion paradigm is ill-suited to understanding the complexities inherent for black mothers because it obscures the intersecting effects of gender and race oppression in their lives. To increase our understandings of the problems faced by mothers, assumptions about collusion must be rigorously unpacked and rooted in an analysis of multiple oppressions to assess the impact on mothers' emotions.

In many respects the ambiguities and contradictions embodied in mothers' emotions need to be explored with women to gain insights into their capacities to develop the empathy necessary for responding in a supportive way to their children. Insight into mothers' feelings as expressed through their emotions are vital for illuminating the factors that contribute to their ability to attune empathetically to their children in the aftermath of child sexual abuse. Ultimately, understanding mothers' emotional needs derive insights into their capacities to be a source of support in the recovery process for their children. The pertinent point is that mothers who are resilient and supported have a vital role to play in their children's recovery from abuse. Through unravelling the emotional effects of their children's victimisation on mothers, it may be possible to depict sources of strength and resiliency for them, and more importantly, perhaps, to identify resilient factors that may assist them in being a resource for their children in their recovery. In this way, we can identify the ways mothers may be compromised in their abilities to be a protective resource to their children in the aftermath of abuse. Interrogating the racially gendered dimensions of black mothers' emotional experiences will provide illuminating analyses of how multiple oppressions cohere together to bring about a particular emotional reaction to their children's victimisation that has implications for their help-seeking and protective strategies. In so doing, we can begin to underline the challenges facing practitioners in making interpretations of mothers' behaviour for assessing what personal resources they have available to meet their children's needs without oversimplifying the complexities that are involved.

5 Mothering in the Aftermath of Abuse

In this chapter I will focus on the effects of the abuse on women's mothering. While the previous chapter has been concerned with the consequences of divided loyalty on mothers' emotional responses, I will extend the discussion in this chapter to look at the ways in which women's mothering and caregiving are affected. The central concern here is to explore three core ideas: mothers' coping strategies, the meanings they attach to their mothering, and their support mechanisms in the aftermath of abuse to consider the implications for mothers' caregiving.

Coping Strategies

On discovery of the abuse, mothers in effect have to balance their own emotional needs whilst also having to take care of the emotional needs of their children. It is important to state at the outset that the challenge fundamentally facing mothers is that they have to find the emotional resources to help their children through the recovery process, despite their own struggles to make sense of the abuse for themselves. For this reason, it is important to consider how mothers respond to their children's emotional needs whilst simultaneously balancing their own conflicting emotions. Most crucially, in the aftermath of intrafamilial abuse, the mother-child relationship can be seriously tested and mothers' emotional states will clearly affect the nature of the interactions with their children. For example, Green (1996) noted that some mothers might unconsciously harbour anger at the child for telling or not telling, or for the break up of their marriage or relationship with partners. The arguments have a broad range: some assert that depending on the age of the child, mothers may see their daughters as in some way responsible for the abuse (Back, 1998), thus feeding into the notion of girls' complicity in their abuse (Miller, 1990). Others hold to the belief that if the child in question is a teenage girl, the assumption is that they have done something to put themselves in that situation or they could have done something to stop the abuse if they did not want it to continue. Some commentators even go as far as to suggest that daughters may be seen as competitors for the mothers' personal space, and in dating situations (Joseph, 1991). The point to stress is that some mothers may have complicated and contradictory feelings towards their children which may not be consciously articulated and which they may have difficulties owning (Parker, 1997). Thus, there is the need to understand that any unexamined feelings mothers may hold will pose difficulties for them to remain open and responsive to their children and will significantly interfere with their capacity to create an alliance with them. The larger issue raised here is that unresolved feelings of loss and grief, or anger towards a child, may impair mothers' capacity to empathise with their children. Specifically, mothers need to resolve feelings of loss and grief before they can be an effective source of support to their children in a time of distress.

Another issue of critical importance is that mothers have the difficult task of not only having to deal with their own feelings of pain and anger, but at the same time deal with their children's pain and anger, which may at times be directed towards them (Russell, 1986). It is thought that children may express feelings of anger towards mothers, because they may believe that their mothers knew about the abuse but did nothing about it. It has to be said, however, that in a culture such as ours that is so steeped in mother-blaming children may vent their anger at their mothers rather than their abusers (Jacobs, 1994; Parker, 1997; Caplan, 2000). Somehow it is easier to make mothers, rather than fathers, the scapegoat when anything goes wrong in children's lives.

For the mothers in the study, where children did express anger at them, some reported feelings of discouragement and helplessness in being able to assist them to manage the intense emotions stirred up. This point is illustrated most lucidly by this mother's account:

> My daughter was fourteen at the time she disclosed that my boyfriend was abusing her. At fourteen she is just coming into her own as a young woman. It affected her very badly and she took a lot of her anger out on me. She would go for days without speaking and would withdraw into a shell then just explode into fits of anger. I had to do a lot of work to repair my relationship with her. She is eighteen now and our relationship is still very strained, and it is as if nothing would make it better.

In struggling to make sense of the abuse, these mothers were often weighed down by another set of worries, most significantly their concerns for the long-term effects of the abuse on their children. Mothers were often apprehensive about the problems that their children will encounter in later life and a core concern of theirs had to do with the effects of the abuse on their children's emotional and mental health. Critically, a number of commentators have noted that child sexual abuse frequently has a significant long-term impact on children's mental health (Bagley, 1995; Hooper and Koprowska, 2000). Furthermore, the short and long-term post-traumatic stress symptoms in some children have been well documented in the data on sexual abuse (Bietchman, Zucker, Hood, DaCosta, Akman, and Cassavia, 1992; Peters, 1988; Rowan and Foy, 1993; Rowan, Foy, Rodriguez and Ryan, 1994; Saunders, Villeponteaux, Lipovsky, Kilpatrick, and Veronen, 1992; Wolfe, Sas, and Wekerle, 1994). For example, children may re-experience the event by experiencing recurrent thoughts, flashbacks, and have sudden intrusive sensory memories of the sexual assault, and may also suffer fear, hyperalertness, anxiety, sleep problems, and nightmares (Briere and Ruuntz, 1993; Feiring, Taska, and Lewis, 1996; Irwin, 1996). Moreover, studies have shown clearly that sexual abuse increases distressing and disruptive behaviour in children (Browne and Finkelhor, 1986; Feiring, Taska, and Lewis, 1996). Mothers described that such problems were present for a number of the children and not surprisingly, they worried about the enduring impact of the abuse on their children's emotional and psychological well-being.

Probably one of the most challenging aspects for mothers was that they clearly did not understand their children's behavioural and developmental needs in the aftermath of abuse. It was clear from their accounts that some mothers were coping with their children displaying what were obviously post-traumatic stress disorder symptoms that were unfamiliar to them. Mothers' anxieties thus surfaced in the ways they responded to their children. More typically, mothers at first perceived their children's behaviour to be disruptive or attention-seeking and therefore some mothers reported responding harshly to their children in order to manage their behaviour, which in turn exacerbated feelings of guilt.

The mother of a nine-year-old girl who was abused by her boyfriend said:

Her behaviour deteriorated and, I'm afraid to say, it would get to the point where I just couldn't stand being around her. She would cry and cry for hours, and when she was not crying she would be withdrawn, angry, and sullen. And I just couldn't stand it anymore. I would sometimes have these outbursts and shout at her, then feel guilty. I would say to her afterwards, even if I've been shouting, no matter how loud I'm shouting it's not the end of the world. I wasn't coping at all.

For the most part, mothers must struggle on their own to deal with the complex needs and demanding behaviour of their children following abuse. Some had little real input from anyone to help them understand the meaning behind their children's behaviour.

A recurring theme in the research is that mothers' parenting following discovery is largely influenced by the nature of her relationship with the abuser. As pointed out in the previous chapter, a number of mothers reported experiencing conflicting emotions and ambivalent feelings towards their partner when he was the perpetrator. Clearly, this resulted in problems in how they mothered their children for ultimately, the costs in some situations, was to jeopardise their relationship with their children. If mothers were able to confront abusers immediately on discovery, they reported feeling better able to foster empathy ties with their children and understand their emotional needs. From this analysis, several points can be drawn out about the implications for children. Most importantly, how do they ensure the interest of their children remain paramount. In essence, mothers have to attune empathetically and validate their children's experiences in order to effectively deal with the ensuing effects on them. Where mothers expressed ambivalence about the relationship with their partners, this limited their capacities for connecting empathetically to their children. It is open to question whether they inadvertently distanced themselves emotionally from their children. Emotional distance is unhelpful for mothers because it is a significant inhibitor to empathic identification, which is a core dimension of good mothering.

Children need a positive nurturing environment to make sense of their traumatic experiences in the aftermath of abuse in order to begin to heal from the effects of the abuse. Certainly, children cannot be expected to know why they have been abused and supportive mothers have a key role to play in being able to help them name and acknowledge the painful reality of abuse. Non-abusing mothers need to be able to attune empathetically to their children, to understand how the sexual abuse has violated the core of the child's being. It is well evidenced by research that emotional support from a sensitive non-abusing significant carer can be a primary mitigating factor in enabling children's recovery from trauma (Spacarelli and Kim, 1995). By enhancing the likelihood that they experience a positive and nurturing environment, mothers can foster

57

resiliency in their children (San Miguel, Morrison and Weissglass, 1995). However, the resultant stressors created in the aftermath of intrafamilial child sexual abuse can affect how mothers are able to deal with their children. Essentially, for some mothers the stress brought to their relationship with their partners on discovery of abuse may mean a drain on their energies at a time when their children demands an intense attention; which mothers may not be able to give. The ensuing turmoil mean that mothers absorbed with their own confused feelings and unmet needs were blocked in their ability to provide a nurturing environment for their children because they had little emotional space for them.

A mother of a six-year-old girl who was abused by her maternal grandfather recalls.

> I now accept that my daughter was angry with me for sending her to stay with my parents, where her grandfather repeatedly abused her – my father. However, at the time it was as if I was shutting of my emotions. By not being able to feel, I would not have to think about what I had to do. But deep down I knew that by shutting off myself, I was creating a wall between my daughter and me.

The mother of a seven-year-old girl who was abused by a close friend of the family had this to say:

> I was doing no more that just holding it together – getting the children to school, taking care of everyone, you know, making sure they had food, went to bed on time, that kind of thing. All the time, though, I was in a state of numbness. I was using so much energy just keeping myself together that I was physically and mentally exhausted and did not have time for my daughter emotionally. In truth, I did not know how to deal with my daughter's feelings so could not give her the attention she deserved.

Clearly, it is here that we can begin to understand some of the mothers' struggles to cope. An important ramification for children is that mothers caught up in their own turbulence may not be able to discern which behaviours in a child require professional advice. The danger here for the children involved is that they might be left to struggle on their own in silence, which can lead to irreparable damage. It was clear from a number of mother's accounts that no one had talked to the children about what had happened to them. As Wyatt (1997) notes, the worst thing that can happen to a child who has been abused is to leave him or her unsupported to deal with the effects by themselves. The ability of mothers to convey to their children that their needs matter takes on a crucial importance in the recovery process for the children. For the mothers keen to help their children through the emotional experience of the abuse grasping the importance of this is a critical factor.

A further complexity is that some mothers' coping was powerfully influenced by family arrangements in their households. For example, a key factor worth highlighting is that single-headed households were over-represented in the sample and these mothers' boyfriends or male partners, not the children's biological fathers, were overwhelmingly the abusers of their children. A slight majority of the mothers, seventeen out of the thirty mothers in the sample, were in single-headed household at the time of the abuse. Though these mothers were parenting alone, some were involved in long or short-term relations with the man who abused their child. The way these mothers described their relationships suggests that they were involved with men who were practically living in their homes, or certainly spending a great deal of time in their households; thus occupying a position of power and authority over their children, but who may not have adopted a formal parenting role involving nurturance and care of their children.

Here, a mother whose twelve-year-old daughter was abused by her boyfriend who disclosed to a teacher at her school offered this perspective:

> We had been going out together for about nine months. We are not living together but he spends a lot of time here – he basically comes and goes as he pleases. He did not get into being like a dad to my two children because they already had their dad who they see quite regularly, so he was more like a friend to them.

This tendency is of course not limited to black mothers. The types of family arrangements for all families and the "parenting" provided by significant others is something that has changed radically in the past thirty years or so for all families regardless of racial or class background. However, research shows that African-Caribbean mothers are more likely to be cohabiting or in a female headed household (Phoenix, 1990). The relevance here for considering these issues is that research highlights that children are particularly vulnerable to sexual abuse from stepfathers and other trusted male authority figures in their lives (Glaser and Frosh, 1988). This point is worthy of consideration as it may be that some abusive men target single mothers to gain access to children, as has been suggested by some commentators (Russell, 1983 and 1985).

It is open to question whether an added dimension for black children is that they are disproportionately more likely to be living with non-biological father-figures, i.e. in relationships with adult males who are not playing a positive significant role in their lives. Lest I give the impression that mothers are deliberately putting their children at risk due to their lifestyle choices, let me state from the outset that this is not my intention. Obviously, it is not possible to generalise about this situation from the data gathered here and clearly, it would be misleading to suggest that. Rather, I am seeking to make visible the multiple experiences of black children in their household arrangements and most importantly to illuminate the complexities inherent in their household situations. To some extent, mothers have to negotiate a new male authority figure into the family unit, who may have an ambiguous role towards their children, but nevertheless is in a position of power over their children. James (2000) makes the point convincingly that whilst black men may exert little economic control over family life, nevertheless they retain considerable physical, sexual and psychological dominance. Depending on the dynamics of the mother-boyfriend relationship, it may be that mothers in the throes of a new relationship who introduce a new member to the household do not have undivided positive attention to give to their children. These factors can create particular stressors on the family unit with mothers becoming estranged from their children. Mothers may have a poor quality of relationship with their children, become alienated from them and indeed; children may experience instability in these situations. Thus, for children, feelings of vulnerability will increase, which may affect their ability to tell their mothers of the abuse when it occurs. Mothers blame themselves and essentially do not have a clear grasp of the ways that abusers groom and coerce child victims and in the process, can effectively destroy a child's relationship of trust with mothers (Morris, 1999). As Nelson (1998) observes the enforcement of silence has been and remains the most powerful weapon of abusers, both individually and collectively.

It is thought that mothers with little emotional space for their children could contribute to children being unable to tell them about the abuse. For instance, Wyatt (1997) notes that girls are less likely to tell their mothers about being abused even if it is their father, stepfather or mother's boyfriend who is the abuser. The strength of their relationship with their children depends largely on the relational process of family problem solving and coping and also, in part upon the stability of mothers' relationships with their children (Thornton and Carter, 1986). All these issues must be unpacked to identify the factors that knit together to create emotional distance between mothers and their children, which also contribute to the vulnerability of some children. In short, without interrogating the additional factors that may make black children vulnerable to abusive men, it would be impossible to illuminate the paramountcy of issues that constrain and inhibit the quality of mothers' caregiving in the aftermath of abuse. The challenge for mothers is how their coping strategies constrain or hinder them in maintaining a relationship with their children in the context of abuse.

Meanings

In this section I shall explore the meanings mothers attached to their mothering and its impact on their coping. Suffice it to say a major impact of the abuse on mothers was to heavily influence how they saw themselves as mothers. Ultimately, this led some to doubt their mothering skills and capacities. Important to grasp is that these mothers lay a particular emphasis on how they see their mothering. Most significantly, the immediate aftermath of discovery engenders a feeling of loss of self-worth, and some mothers were imbued with a sense of their own failure. The significance of this needs to be understood in a context where so much of their sense of self-worth and esteem as women is strongly connected with how they see themselves as mothers (Hill Collins, 1997). Accordingly, women's expectations of what it is to be a good mother influenced their emotional state in the aftermath of the abuse. This in turn meant how mothers internalise ideas of maternal failure overwhelmingly influenced their emotional coping.

The mother of a nine-year-old girl who was abused by her father said this:

> You hear about these things happening – you sometimes hear whispers in the neighbourhood about so and so family up the road – but you never think it would happen in your family – right under my nose and I did not know. It had to take my daughter acting out at school for it to come to light. As a mother, one of the things I prided myself on was that my children could talk to me, you know, could confide in me. I feel I have hurt my daughter. It has been very difficult to talk to anyone about these things, and sometimes I know that it didn't help my daughter or me.

61

For many of the mothers, reaffirming the centrality of their nurturing role preoccupied them. Insofar as mothers want to do what is best for their children, their lack of support coupled with isolation led some to question their failure to provide consistent and nurturing care to their children.

This mother, for example, whose eight-year-old daughter was abused by her partner comments:

> It must have been very stressful for my daughter. I wanted to know what had happened, how many times it happened, all the gory details, things like that. I'd be asking a lot of questions. I'd be always checking her out. If she was having a bath or something, I would be checking up on her. I don't know what I was looking for. It was as if I wanted to satisfy myself that I did not do anything wrong as a mother. Poor child – she never expressed what she was going through.

To better understand mothers' distress, it is necessary to consider the ways in which cultural forces shape their perception of motherhood and child-rearing. Expectations about child-rearing are racially and culturally rooted and powerfully influenced how mothers see their mothering (Hill Collins, 1990). One might argue that this is the case for all parents. However, for black mothers, parenting within a racist culture means there are some essential messages that they must impart to their children to shore up aspects of well-being, including their racial and gendered identity. A continuing struggle for black mothers is striving to raise well-adjusted children with a strong sense off self-esteem in a society that stigmatises them brings many challenges (Greene, 1990; Robinson, 1995; Staples, 1994). Thus, mothers' expectations for their children and their priorities will significantly shape their parenting strategies and goals (Hill and Sprague, 1999; Reynolds, 1997). Take the task of facilitating the cognitive abilities and social and emotional development of their children, for example. For black mothers, in terms of developing resiliency in their children, they must parent their children to resist the racism that devalues their humanity and constantly denigrates them, whilst simultaneously successfully readying them to adapt to the majority cultural values (Dove, 1998). Indeed, that mothers must teach their children from an early age about social belonging in their community is accorded primacy as an aid to the development of a coherent sense of self in a society that inscribes a marginal social status to them. Another significant difference for black mothers is that they contribute to their daughters' gender identity development in a unique way by explicitly teaching them to be economically independent to reflect the fact that race and class will profoundly shape their material reality (Phoenix, 1990). Hence, it could be argued that these women are already mothering under conditions that are less than ideal.

Most explicitly, the task of mothering in the best of circumstances presents numerous obstacles. However, compounded with the experiences of abuse, these mothers face an uphill struggle in helping their children heal from the effects of the abuse. Indeed, concern for how their children will internalise the abusive experiences preoccupied mothers. One of mothers' concerns therefore, centred on whether their children would internalise the abusive experience as part of their black identity. Important to emphasise is that black children may believe that they were abused because they are black, or that abuse only happens in black families (Droisen, 1989; Hudson, 1992; Jackson, 1996). One possible explanation is that in the context of racism, black children may have difficulties unravelling whether their feelings of worthlessness (something experienced by children who have been abused) may be due to the abuse or racism (Droisen, 1989). Additionally, it is thought that black children may be doubly traumatised by the experience of coping with racism and being abused by someone from their own racial or cultural background (Jackson, 1996). These were important considerations the mothers were grappling with, since they perceive it reflects on them when anything goes wrong in their children's lives.

Therefore, careful attention has to be given to these concerns to pinpoint the extra hurdles black mothers have to overcome in ensuring their children recover from the abuse psychologically intact. Fundamentally, to assist their children in developing a healthy sense of self in the aftermath of abuse, they essentially have to be able to contribute in a positive way to the emotional resources that can enhance their children's resiliency and coping. However, mothers' own resiliency factors might be impaired due to their circumstances. As I noted earlier, mothers' own needs, wants, and interests will significantly influence their ability to respond appropriately to their children's needs. Meanwhile, they have to continue to find ways to support their children by themselves, by whatever means they can.

Another area of contention centres on the social assumptions about black motherhood that are rooted in racially stigmatising myths of them as deficit mothers. In other words, these ideas affected them in their perceptions of how others might view them. Essentially, racism means that black women's mothering is socially devalued and as such, they are not starting out on a level playing field; their mothering is measured against a standard set by others. Paradoxically, African-Caribbean mothers are viewed as strict and authoritarian, yet poor at providing boundaries and consistent care and discipline (Robinson, 1995). Therefore, for black mothers, the analogy of the harsh yet neglectful mother is one that is hard to dispel. Additionally, negative stereotypes of black women's sexuality impinge upon and influence how mothers are seen (Marshall, 1994). For example, the subtle assumptions that black women are loose and sexually promiscuous underpin the respective value others place on their mothering and reinforce perceptions of them as worthless mothers.

When sexual abuse occurs in their families, these concerns have particular resonance with mothers, in the way perceptions of how others might view them dominate their thinking. An added complexity for these women is that mothering in a context with many external-devaluing messages plays a critical role in how they come to see themselves as inferior parents on discovery of abuse in their families. The charge of "putting their daughters at risk" by exposing them to different men in their homes was not far from some mothers thinking. In brief, given the cultural milieu of black women's parenting these mothers were acutely aware of the shame and stigma attached to their children's abuse and felt that this somehow marked them out as being at fault and therefore as failed mothers and open to charges of a lack of maternal care. Not surprisingly, mothers therefore had concerns about coming up for harsh scrutiny and particularly feared others would judge them negatively. For some of the mothers, their deep-rooted beliefs that it is their responsibility as mothers to protect their children aroused intense feelings of anxiety. These feelings became most acute when they lost confidence in their abilities to parent, which provoked a crisis of identity for a number of mothers. But by far a mother's greatest struggle is that her daily functioning amidst negative valuations requires high levels of motivation, commitment and support (Genero, 1998).

For some though, perhaps because the disclosure was made to someone else this evoked powerful emotions for then about their mothering skills and fed into internalised ideas of the "good" and "bad" mother.

Eighteen months after disclosure this mother was still blaming herself that she had not picked up on the signs that her boyfriend was abusing her seven-year-old daughter:

Looking back I can remember her coming home and saying that her genitals were itching, and me saying that she hadn't washed properly. And I remember laying her down and having a look at her vagina but I didn't see anything that looked outrageous or different, or made me think someone had been interfering with her. Obviously, now I'd know what I was looking for and what it meant. It is still running round in my head that she was trying to tell me that she was being abused and I didn't hear, I didn't see. I suppose, yes, I am still blaming myself.

The implicit assumption here seems to be the all-knowing omnipotent mother who has the ability to protect the child from any harm (Jacobs, 1994). Additionally, for some of the mothers the discovery of the violation of their children may have stirred up their own unresolved issues of being parented. In particular, it powerfully put some in touch with their experiences of being mothered.

Here one mother whose daughter was abused by her brother and the child disclosed to the mothers' best friend recounts:

Certainly, my own mother was emotionally distant.......I felt as the eldest child that I was picking up many of her problems. I pledged to myself that I would not raise my child the way my mother raised me. I was going to be better, more loving, provide more mothering and all that kind of stuff. It was quite a shock when my daughter could not talk to me about her abuse.

As we can see from this example, not only was this mother deeply hurt that her child could not talk with her, but the discovery stirred up powerful feelings about her own experiences of being mothered. What we have here is a situation whereby the disclosure of her daughter's abuse was to bring to the surface unresolved feelings of her childhood relationship with her mother. This mother was forced to revisit tensions and concerns from her own childhood and her daughter's abuse jolted her to recall her experiences of being mothered, and in particular the atmosphere of her upbringing and how being cast as a substitute mother has influenced her mothering. The circumstances of her own childhood came flooding back to her in a very painful way to remind her of the wish not to recreate the kind of mother-daughter relationship that she had with her own mother. In the process of grieving the loss she experienced on discovery of her daughter's abuse, this mother was also ostensibly grieving a loss from her own childhood, notably her own experiences of being mothered.

65

For the small number of mothers of children who were disabled, there was additional emotional turmoil about the meaning of their mothering. Especially because their children had an abused status to add to the other stigmatised identities as disabled black children, mothers' feelings of inferiority and marginalisation were compounded. These mothers' concerns arose out of a belief that the abuse of disabled children is given less weight by society as a whole, and thus influenced child protection workers' views (Westcott and Cross, 1996; Sinason, 2000). This seems a telling point, and some mothers felt little understood when they attempted to bring their concerns to child protection agencies.

In this mother's words:

> My daughter who has a learning disability resided with foster carers during the weekdays and spent weekends at home with me. I began to suspect that something had happened to Tanya when her behaviour changed. It took a long time for the authorities to take my concerns seriously and I felt it had to do with the fact that my daughter has a learning disability. The behaviour my daughter was displaying that alerted me that something was wrong was initially put down to her disability. I had to keep insisting that something was wrong and that an investigation needed to take place. I felt a deep sense of anger and stigma. At the same time, I also felt very guilty. At the time, I thought if she was home with me full-time this would not have happened. I blame myself... and the funny thing is that I feel my mother also blames me. It was as if my daughter was being punished for my wanting support to help raise her.

This example illustrates the suppressed rage and mixed feelings felt by this mother. Two points emerge from this example. First, the way this mother was acutely aware that negative valuation of a black disabled child compounded the invisibility of her experiences and left her feeling that her child was not worthy of serious consideration. Evidentiary standards for the abuse of children with disabilities are different than for non-disabled children and this mother was acutely aware of these subtle processes that further stigmatised her daughter. Second, what is elucidated is the ways multiple forms of marginalised identities interact to mean that denial and a lack of support accompany the reporting of sexual abuse of black disabled children (Bernard, 1999). This mother was left in no doubt that the intersecting effects of race and disability discrimination influenced social services response to her daughter. Thus, it is revealing that despite this mother's extreme anger at the abuser and the child protective system, she nevertheless assumed some responsibility for her daughter's abuse, thus intensifying the complex emotions and reinforcing feelings of guilt.

Support

In the rest of this chapter I will look at how the mothers made use of formal and informal networks to support their parenting in the aftermath of abuse. As noted earlier, how well-supported mothers felt influenced their interpersonal strategies for coping. A key finding of the research is that many mothers resorted to their own social networks of support rather than seek out formal support systems such as child protection services. Where formal helping services were involved, this tended to happen where the abuse came to light through the child disclosing to someone at school and rarely on the mothers' instigation. For a small number of mothers with supportive networks of extended kin, the emotional sustenance from significant others in their lives were a critical factor in bolstering their resiliency. It is well documented that some of the primary factors that strengthened mothers' resilience are supportive social networks, good extended family helping arrangements, and a strong sense of self (McAdoo, 1998). These factors will not only determine the level of resiliency of mothers but also shape the help-seeking process (McGubbin, Futrell, Thompson and Thompson, 1998). Especially, the strength in mothers' support networks not only afforded them with an opportunity to talk openly about their feelings, but also equipping them to examine their options.

The role of family and kin as protective shields against abusive men was highlighted as a means for some mothers in helping them to confront their children's abusers. They emphasised the role of supportive nurturing relatives as being of ultimate importance in giving them the courage to confront abusive men; something the mothers with poor support networks felt unable to do.

Here the mother of a nine-year-old girl who was abused by a male relative sums up her feelings:

> With the help of my sister, I was able to go round to his house and confront him in front of his wife. It took a lot of courage, because in the early days I had a lot of uncertainties and doubts. But seeing the effect it was having on my daughter convinced me that I was doing the right thing. He denied it and both him and his wife tried to make out that it was not true and I was being spiteful, but it helped me to feel I wasn't

67

keeping quiet about it. Somehow having my sister there to talk it through with gave me the strength to act.

In this instance, this mother's support networks served as a coping device for her. Though it was not easy for this mother, by drawing strength from her sister's support, she was able to feel empowered to challenge the abuser, thus implicitly giving a powerful message of alliance with her daughter.

Therefore, it seems a key factor for mothers' resiliency was the need to have relationships that supported and sustained them. In essence, it was those mothers who drew on informal support networks such as relatives that were the key determinants underlying their resiliency. Again, it is useful to examine the ways this not only acted as a cushion to help mothers withstand the impact of the abuse but, it helped some to be emotionally resilient to support their children to effectively deal with the stressors that will ensue for them as a result of the trauma. Particularly, mothers that were able to draw on the support of extended and wider community networks seemed much more tuned in to their children's emotional needs. Primarily, these mothers were able to utilise family bonds as a resource to bolster their own resiliency and by implications their children's resiliency.

For example, this mother explained:

I made available to my daughter people who she could talk to, who would listen to her. In view of the abuse she suffered, I felt it was important to create safe environments for her to talk. I saw my role as pointing her in the right direction. And because of the way I found my family to be very supportive, which cleared the way for me to use them to help my daughter to talk.

However, it would appear that mothers felt much more able to call on family for support when the abuser was not a blood relative. One possible explanation is that when families are not related to the perpetrator, it lessens the chances of them experiencing mixed feelings of loyalty.

Concern for the well-being of others influenced some mothers' decisions whether to tell their families or not. This mother found it difficult to tell other members of her family that her husband had abused their daughter because of concerns that they would be burdened with something unpleasant.

When I first told my mother, I was very ashamed... I suppose I wanted to protect her, and I didn't want to deal with her reactions. I was never able to talk openly about sexual topics with my mother, and even though I was now a grown woman, I was still affected by that. I was very uncomfortable. It wasn't like I couldn't discuss it with her.. In the end I just said: I know someone whose daughter was sexually abused. But my mother knew immediately that I was talking about my situation.

In contrast, the mothers who did not have supportive networks around them tell a very different story. Some mothers, however, adopted the strategy of hiding the abuse from family and friends, because of feelings of fear and shame. The mother of an eight-year-old girl who was abused by her stepfather had this to say:

Had I realised that at the time, I would have been bright enough to phone my mother and get her support. But I didn't. I didn't tell her. She doesn't know. My daughter's father doesn't know either. That's something about me, I realise now, but I didn't then.

Following the disclosure that her stepfather had been sexually abusing her daughter, this mother felt unable to talk to her own family:

I did not talk to many people about it, only a close friend who had been through something similar. In many ways I did not know whom to trust to talk honestly about it. My family did not like my husband, and I felt telling them would only confirm their views of him. But I also felt the more people that knew, the more likely she (my daughter) is going to be marked out.

When contrasted with those mothers who had good support networks, the mothers with little emotional resources and support struggled to help their children through the recovery process. At worst, the mothers without support did not have avenues for renewal and solace to replenish their waning energies. Ultimately, the abuse remains shrouded in secrecy, as these mothers in effect have to lie to themselves, to their families, and most importantly to their children. As I previously noted, for some mothers pressure from families to not involve anyone outside the family compounded feelings of isolation and affected their help-seeking strategies. A further problem arises for mothers, for in the absence of confiding relationships they floundered and continued to be plagued with self-blame for their children's abuse.

Discussion

So how are we to interpret women's mothering in the aftermath of abuse. As indicated throughout this chapter, the issue of women's mothering with all its ambiguities and contradictions in the aftermath of abuse pose certain problems of interpretations. As a deeper understanding of mothers' resiliency mechanisms and coping strategies is sought assessing whether the mothering black women provide in the aftermath of sexual abuse is "good enough" is a complex and multi-layered process. As we have seen in this chapter, a number of issues arise for mothers in the aftermath of abuse. Most noticeably, major stressors provide significant challenges for mothers and essentially impede their capacity to mother competently. Above all, concern for their children's long-term developmental needs contributed considerably to these mothers' emotional distresses and impacted their mothering in a most profound way. In short, what emerged very strongly was that some mothers were often left to struggle alone with how best to respond to their children's needs and interests with little support from anyone. It is important, therefore, to recognise that in the aftermath of abuse, race and gender factors intersect for black mothers to mean in effect they are parenting in a context of hostility, anger, conflict and loss.

In many ways, the mothers who sought help, whether from formal or informal networks of support, were subjecting their parenting to a critical scrutiny. Therefore, the primacy of listening to mothers, but especially listening non-judgementally has to be emphasised. Mothers need to have a safe space to explore the doubts and concerns they inherently struggle with, without the fear of blame. Yet, professional helpers need to listen without relying on assumptions of the "deficient" or "collusive" mother and importantly, without loosing sight of children's needs and rights.

The final point that is important to emphasise is that ultimately, what interpersonal resources mothers draw upon to enhance coping is influenced by their own resiliency mechanisms. It is well to keep in mind that lived experiences affect resilience and coping mechanisms. Such consideration highlights the importance of recognising that black mothers' parenting strategies are deeply embedded in their gendered and racial backgrounds, which will influence the modes of coping that they develop.

As I discussed in chapter four, mothers' coping strategies are heavily influenced by race and gender dynamics that determine the types of stressors they encounter on discovery; but especially, mothers' appraisal of stress will influence their coping strategies and help-seeking. But perhaps, most importantly mothers' fear of racism can be a barrier to expressing feelings of pain and distress around the abuse (Ahmed and Webb-Johnson, 1995), and by implications this will also hinder their abused children's ability to express their feelings. Essentially, what emotional resources mothers provide their children with will be influenced by their own ways of coping and surviving. Therefore, to appraise the choices mothers make for their children, it is necessary to understand how the combined effects of oppression and devaluation serve to circumscribe mothers' caregiving. These are the starting points through which women's mothering and subsequent coping ought to be evaluated.

6 Balancing Needs and Risks

In this chapter, mothers' help-seeking behaviour is explored further to draw out some implications for identifying risk factors for their children. Centrally, this chapter traces the inherent tensions in understanding the conflicts for mothers balanced against the safety and long term emotional needs of their children. Drawing on some of the themes addressed in chapters four and five, some wider questions concerning how we can develop a coherent understanding for carrying out risk assessments for black children are broached.

Individual Risk Situations for Black Children

For social work practitioners, whose primary responsibility lies with promoting the welfare of children, the question of how best to make sound judgements about mothers' decision-making and help-seeking patterns is imperative. While it is important for practitioners to understand the meanings underlying mothers' behaviours, nonetheless, problematic questions are raised about the paramountcy of the children's needs, insofar as children have their own unique needs and interests, which may at times be in conflict with the interests of their mothers. In reality, child protection workers have to recognise potential and actual conflict that may have a negative impact on the children involved, so that they are not disadvantaged by their mothers' actions. Fundamentally, without undermining mothers' coping strategies, practitioners not only have to assess mothers' needs, but they also have to look critically at child protection issues to identify behaviours in mothers that may pose a risk to children's safety and long term emotional needs. Given these dilemmas, what criteria will be used to judge mothers' actions? Let us consider that practitioners have to make professional decisions as to whether a mother has the capacity to empathise with her child and protect him or her from further abuse. The situation requires assessing standards of acceptable parenting and making estimations about whether mothers' strategies for coping may in fact leave their children exposed to further harm. In assessing mothers' capacity to care safely for their children, sensitive questioning is critical to elicit the necessary information that is vital for making skilful decisions, not only about the quality of the parenting, but

72

also the interaction between mothers and their children. It is from this frame of reference that practitioners can begin to weigh up the issues that are involved in balancing the safety needs, rights, and interests of children against the needs and responsibilities of their mothers.

Paying rigorous attention to children's needs and refraining from mother-blaming is a difficult path to tread. For practitioners striving to work from an anti-oppressive standpoint, conflicts of interests between children's and mothers' needs may be especially difficult to discern and essentially, assessment of "good enough" mothering will hinge on mothers' willingness to put the best interest of their children above their own needs. Practitioners must also be attentive to the factors that can present obstacles in mothers' way to secure their children's safety. Reconciling the needs and interests of children and those of their mothers can create a tension and ultimately children may not receive the type of care they have a right to expect from their carers. Thus, in balancing needs it is important to ascertain mothers' conceptualisation of their children's safety and emotional needs. Similarly, mothers' understandings of risk are critical as a starting point for making assessments about their ability to protect their children from further harm. Principally, practitioners struggling to comprehend the nuances of black mothers' experiences will have to examine mothers' behaviours to understand what reactions may stem from coping strategies developed for survival in a racist society, but at the same time explore whether some of that behaviour may be endangering their children's safety.

In assessing present and future risks to children, how will practitioners be satisfied that mothers have their children's best interest and safety needs at heart? Here, for example, one mother whose twelve-year-old daughter was abused by her male cohabitee had this to say about her reasons for not disclosing to anyone outside the family:

> At the time it felt like the right thing to do – not to go to the authorities.... I had many doubts about whether it was the best thing to do. I spent days, weeks, it seems wondering what to do for the best. As time went by I felt they (social services) would have wondered why it took me so long to report it. I thought they might have felt I had something to hide....To be honest, you hear of so many of the black families on the estate who are having difficulties with social services....Some families have kids going in and out of care and nothing much seems to be changing for these children and their families. I did not want that happening to my daughter. The trust was not there and I was also very frightened.

Efforts to make judgements about the risks attached to mothers' behaviours and a child being at continuing risk will pose the most difficult challenge for practitioners. It is possible to argue that some mothers' actions might strengthen their children's safety and resiliency. On the other hand, we also need to be alert to the possibility that others might indeed shape the very vulnerability of the children (McCubbin, Futrell, Thompson, and Thompson, 1998). These are critical factors to take into account in deciding which of mothers' actions pose a risk of significant harm. However, it is important to remember that finding ways to intervene sensitively and appropriately with black children for ensuring that their interests remain at the centre should be the overall goal. Although mothers' fears need to be appreciated and handled sensitively, at the same time, children's vulnerability should be the predominate concern.

To refer back briefly to the ideas expounded in chapters four and five, my argument is that a number of factors intersect to make it difficult for mothers to hear, see, and know of their children's abuse. Thus, in considering risk situations for black children, the factors that can inhibit them from telling their mothers, and more importantly, their mothers' ability to listen and hear, need to be understood in order to make evaluative judgements about risk and mother's capacities to respond appropriately to their children's needs. For instance, a number of mothers in the study revealed how hurt they felt that their children did not disclose to them and found it difficult to talk to them about the abuse. Clearly, the quality of the mother-child relationship before the abuse will be a contributory factor in how their children relate to them in the aftermath of abuse. However, that their children found it difficult to speak to them may not be that dissimilar to other groups of children from different racial backgrounds. What may be different for black children is the significant role racism plays in shaping their perception of why they were abused thus making it difficult for them to verbalise their experiences; because the shame that they are already feeling on account of being black is compounded by the experience of abuse (Thomas, 2000). Indeed, it is thought that racism can have a direct impact on how black children tell their parents of the occurrence of abuse and how they make sense of their experiences in the aftermath of abuse (Jackson, 1996). The negative construction of black children's identity may present them with difficulties in how they give voice to their experiences of victimisation, particularly when it occurs within their own families. All these factors operate to silence black children from speaking of the abuse to their mothers and ultimately affect their closeness and level of support. It is thought that black children may be especially fearful that disclosure of the abuse outside the family would bring shame and unhappiness to their mothers (Droisen, 1989). Perhaps, ironically, black children also struggle with feelings of disloyalty to their families if they disclose to outsiders.

These experiences underscore the difficulties black children will be faced with, and in particular, their immediate and long term emotional needs can go unmet. We know from research that if children's needs are not responded to appropriately and they are not allowed to grieve childhood trauma this can have long-term effects on their emotional development (Falberg, 1982). Making explicit the processes involved for black children in how they disclose and talk about their experiences offer insights into how they develop coping skills to adapt to their unsafe situations. Thus, a balance needs to be struck between understanding the factors that might obstruct mothers' abilities to respond appropriately to their children whilst at the same time making sure that their needs do not overshadow children's rights and safety needs. Perhaps more importantly, taking mothers' concerns seriously means finding ways to tease out the effects of the abuse on their parenting without jeopardising children's emotional well-being and safety needs. Yet keep in mind that children are the ones without the voice and have the least choice about remaining in an environment that is harmful to their emotional well-being (Alleyne, 1997; Hollies, 1990).

The Question of Silence

The issue concerning those mothers who tell no one about the abuse begs an absolutely vital question about complicity. To what extent would these mothers' decisions to keep quiet be taken as an indication of their collusion with abusers, thus posing a risk to their children? Undoubtedly, the question of silence raises concerns about actual and potential risks to children's future safety needs. These are particularly critical points to consider, for the question of silence ultimately challenges practitioners to consider whether they are dealing with complicity or merely women's uncertainties about the reception they will receive should they seek help from social services.

Key findings from the research suggest that the shame felt by some mothers made them reluctant to seek help from anyone. Some were especially reluctant to involve social services because of their fear of loosing their children. This excerpt from a mother whose daughter was abused by her partner highlights the doubts some mothers can experience around their decisions not to report the abuse to child protection services:

> I mean, I couldn't say I was very clear about what I was doing. The stress and worry was draining me, and I just couldn't face anyone. At the time I felt I was doing the right thing and protecting my daughter (and the rest of the family) by not going to the authorities. They (social workers) just have such a negative attitude towards black people and that did not make me want to go and talk to them. I felt they would be asking a lot of questions – questions, at the time, I couldn't even face myself. I took steps to make sure my daughter was not abused again. I made sure he (my ex-partner) was not allowed back into the house, and that she (and my other two children) did not go anywhere near him. I couldn't bear to speak to my daughter though. I couldn't cope with hearing what she had gone through. I felt the best thing was for her to not talk about it, that way she would be able to forget it and get on with her life. It is only now that I have had some distance that I can see that my daughter would have benefited from some professional help. It destroyed my relationship with my daughter. I feel she has only hate and anger towards me now.

This account call attention to how complex the issues are for mothers to make sense of their reasons for not seeking professional help. For a number of mothers this realisation put them in touch with their own coping patterns and its impact on their ability to break the silence about their children's abuse. The mother of a nine-year-old girl who was abused by her husband made the following comments:

> This is the first time I have really spoken to anyone about my daughter's abuse. I couldn't begin to explain what had been going on to the rest of my family....No one wanted to know - you know what some of us are like in our community – "it does not happen here". This makes you not trust anyone anymore – not even my own family. So that made it even more difficult to find the words to talk about what I was feeling. My life fell apart, and I was crying all the time. I was very fearful about going to social services. I felt that the finger would be pointed at me – you know being the mother, it must be something I am not doing right. I did not want to loose my children....At the same time I was filled with doubts and all the time, asking myself how come I did not know. I supposed I coped by "switching" off most of the time.

Another mother gives an example that speaks of how the silencing nature of shame, secrecy, and denial impacted her ability to acknowledge her daughter's abuse. This mother whose fourteen-year-old daughter was abused by the leader of the church youth group she belonged to had this to say:

> I found it difficult even to say it out loud to myself. I could not think how to begin to talk to anyone else about it. It was as if I spoke about it that would make it seem real – you know, the reality of it would have sunk home. Looking back, I think she had tried to talk to me about what was going on but I never realised what she was trying to tell me. She finally told a teacher at her school, but later denied that anything had happened. I was very concerned that it would become widely known in our church, so did not want to discuss it with anyone. I was too ashamed and there were times when I was not even sure whether I believed my daughter or not. We have never had a very close relationship; in fact we are not a close family at all, in terms of talking openly about our feelings, so that made it even worse.

Here it could be interpreted that this mother seemed more concerned that the abuse did not become known in her church than with the needs of her daughter. There appears to be an absence of concern about the effects of the abuse on her daughter and this raises serious questions about her capacity to consider her daughter's immediate and long-term emotional needs. The impression conveyed is that she is emotionally detached from her daughter and the relationship seems hostile, and worryingly, she appears unable to recognise or empathise with her daughter's pain. It is difficult to say whether this mother's lack of overt expression of concern indicates a lack of empathy. As has been noted earlier, cognitive dissonance may mean there is a marked difference in what a mother may truly feel and what she is able to clearly verbalise. Here, if we assume that this was a mother who had not spoken openly before to anyone about her feelings and dilemmas, then we can begin to understand her difficulties in giving voice to her experiences. In attempting to give an honest account of her feelings, captured are the complex suppressed emotions that impact her capacity to recognise and empathise her with daughter's trauma. This mother was herself sexually abused as a child by her father and had never told anyone about this experience. She went on to recount some of her experiences and particularly her ways of dealing (or not dealing) with her own childhood trauma:

> My father started to sexually abuse me when I was about 12 or 13 – it's all very blurred now, and I don't remember exactly when it started. I have never told anyone about it, but I am sure my mother knew. My mother

and father were pillars of the community, well respected in the church, and I am sure no one would have ever believed me and that this was going on in our family. They instilled in me from a very early age that I should not talk about the family business outside of the family home to anyone. These beliefs are still very much with me and I have passed them on to my daughter. I thought I had dealt with it, you know, I had got over it, because I never talked about it. I felt I did alright and I'm managing to get on with my life....I did well at school, I've got a good job, and I am well respected in my church. I prided myself on being able to cope and function without talking about it to anyone. In fact I always thought that not talking about it is what has helped me to survive on a day-to-day. Finding out about my daughter's abuse has made me realise how much I have not dealt with my own abuse and how much it's affecting my life and my relationship with my daughter.

This example exemplifies the utter complexity of the way secrecy can fuel shame and compound victims' experiences of sexual abuse in black families. One might wonder whether a significant factor for this mother could be that having unresolved issues from her own childhood trauma contributed to her difficulties with prioritising her daughter's needs. She had to confront the reality of her own trauma and reexperience some of the traumatic events, whilst simultaneously having to deal with the consequences of her daughter's abuse. To some extent, the disclosure of her daughter's abuse has forced her to acknowledge her own childhood abuse and this was somewhat getting in the way of establishing an empathic bond with her. It is possible that some mothers who were themselves victimised in childhood may have difficulties recognising and hearing of their children's experience of abuse, because their own coping strategies and defence mechanisms are so interconnected with secrecy and denial. In this case, the combined manifestations of secrecy and denial are indisputably bound together and are likely to be a major factor in this mother's ability to break the silence in order to come to terms with the truth of her own abuse for her self-recovery, before she can even begin the painful process of understanding the impact of sexual abuse on her daughter.

On the surface, mothers' silences may suggest a tacit agreement. Nevertheless, from the point of view of some mothers, the stigma of having your child sexually violated by your partner is powerful and some may feel that they have to struggle and manage on their own – and as one mother in the study put it, "basically shut up and get on with it". As I have pointed out before, the fact that many of the mothers in the study did not tell anyone outside the home about the abuse attests to this reality. This may explain, in part, why some mothers were reluctant to involve child protection services. A recurring theme for a number of mothers was the fear of their children being removed from them, which powerfully affected their perception of the statutory helping processes. It would be too simplistic to suggest that all mothers will automatically be supportive of their children. It may be tempting to assume, or indeed take for granted, that all mothers will be able to straightforwardly face and accept the situation and act in the best interest of their children. This way of thinking obscures a very complex emotional process that renders some mothers unwilling, unable, or not quite ready to engage with the unpalatable truths they need to deal with in order to acknowledge and finally accept the situation (Salt, Myer, Coleman and Sauzier, 1990).

As noted previously, there is not always a linear progression from disclosure to believing, to acceptance, and mothers have to be allowed a grieving process before they can begin to come to grips with the enormity of the situation. Nevertheless, the idea that mothers who tell no one are collusive is a compelling one that is hard to dislodge. Simply to assess the intricate processes mothers go through as complicity is problematic, and belies the significant number of mothers who were struggling with confused feelings and divided loyalties. Notwithstanding, practitioners must also be open to the possibility that there will be some mothers who are not able or willing to accept that their partners may have sexually abused their children and will resist statutory interventions (Salt, Myer, Coleman and Sauzier, 1990). Certainly, it must be borne in mind that some mothers are not able to be supportive of their children and this will be largely influenced by their emotional state, cognitive functioning, and social well-being. Mothers struggling with confused emotions and ambivalent feelings towards their partners may consciously or unconsciously turn their anger onto their children. Indeed, we should be acutely aware that there are instances where children are sometimes not believed, ignored, punished or not supported by non-abusive adults when they disclose abuse (Wyatt and Mickey, 1988; Salt, 1990).

Clearly, it is necessary to understand some of the reasons why some mothers may be reluctant to involve child protection services. However, a mother's own understanding of risk is essential as a starting point for making judgements about her ability to protect her child from further harm. In particular, mothers' perception of the situation is critical for considering how they see their priorities and concerns relating to their children's well-being. To discern why mothers make the choices that they do, we need to examine the constraining factors in their lives to illuminate the powerful injunctions that act to inhibit some black mothers from speaking about their children's abuse and accessing help. In other words, if we are to understand mothers' behaviour, the social norms that perpetuate silence about sexual abuse need to be analysed to bring into full view the barriers to mothers giving voice to their children's abuse. Interrogating the conditions that give rise to mothers' fears and the coping strategies resultant allows for a fuller understanding of the ambivalence for them in breaking the silence about the abuse.

There is a certain paradox in that child protection workers are effectively being asked to respect the veracity of mothers' accounts balanced against powerful and pervasive ideas about "collusive mothers" they may grapple with or hold. In essence, whilst practitioners need to consider the barriers in the path of mothers' speaking out about their children's abuse, they also have a critical role to play in enabling some mothers to confront uncomfortable truths about the abuse, the nature of their relationship with their partners, and significantly the quality of their relationship with their children. Notably, mothers' actions may also present a potential problem from the point of view of children since there are risks attached; it is possible that their actions can mask the emotional harm (perhaps unintentionally) that some children experience on disclosure; for example, children may be accused of making it up, or be pressurised not to talk to anyone else about the abuse. An exploration of the tensions involved in these issues can help practitioners steer a path between mothers' and children's needs, yet at the same time not lose focus on the paramountcy of children's safety needs.

Effects of the Helping Process

There is evidence from the data to show mothers responding empathically to their children but not receiving a supportive service from the helping professionals. Interestingly, the findings suggest that some mothers who sought help to support their children in the aftermath of abuse, found that the expected assistance from the helping professionals cannot always be relied on. Particularly, some mothers reported slowness by professionals in responding to their concerns and what seemed to them a reluctance to intervene. It felt to these mothers that it was as if their status as working-class black women was used to position them as subordinate, and thus mute their legitimate concerns about their children's safety. Not sufficient evidence was often cited as a reason not to do a full investigation in several situations. These women stated that it felt as if the professionals did not deem their children deserving of serious and respectful attention. Mothers reported that though nothing overtly was said, they often felt fobbed off and ultimately left feeling as if the source of the problem lay with their parenting.

The findings show some mothers making repeated attempts to get social services to intervene when they suspected that their children was being sexually abused.

In one case the mother of a twelve-year-old girl with a learning disability became suspicious that someone at her school was molesting her. In recalling her daughter's experience she explains:

My daughter was twelve at the time when I began to suspect that something was wrong. I started to notice drastic changes in her behaviour that to me indicated emotional distress. She was crying all the time, and would become uncontrollable, angry and would masturbate constantly. I first raised my concerns with her teacher at school, but I felt I was fobbed off. I then reported my concerns to the social services child protection team, but was told that her behaviour was due to her disabilities and that it was possible something to do with the fact that she was entering puberty. So the matter was not investigated fully. I had to keep insisting that something be done, and basically, I felt I had to make a nuisance of myself by going to social services repeatedly because by then my daughter's behaviour was getting worse. The professionals labelled me as obsessive, overly anxious and suffering from Munchausen Syndrome by Proxy (at the time I did not know what Munchausen meant, so I did not know they thought I was mad – sick in the head – attention-seeking). But I kept thinking this little black girl, without a voice literally, has to have someone to speak up for her. It took me nearly two years of persistence before professionals would agree to have her medically examined, where it was found that her hymen was not intact – and there were scars on her hymen that were at least two years old. I was left feeling very powerless and under suspicion, and the most hurtful thing was that my parenting was being questioned. It was as if it was me that had done something wrong. It felt to me that because my daughter was a black child with a disability and did not have the language to express what was happening to her, that somehow she was not worthy of any serious attention from the professionals who were there to help.

This example illustrates the efforts of this mother to draw attention to the risks her daughter was exposed to. The professionals involved at the time did not appreciate the concerns and a full assessment of her daughter's circumstances was slow in coming forward. Rather than seeing this mother's response as a positive expression of concern to secure her daughter's safety needs, the reaction to her was to pathologise her and locate the problem firstly with her daughter's disabilities and secondly with attempts to discredit her by questioning her mental stability and parenting abilities. Recognition of the central role this mother was playing in taking action to protect her daughter's safety needs was not acknowledged and utilised as a critical resource for working in the best interest of her daughter. Moreover, this mother's distress was intensified at a time when she had to rely on her own strengths to maintain an assertive stance (an assertive stance that incidentally, was labelled as difficult and obsessive) to secure the protection and well-being of her daughter.

Some mothers recounted that though they had little confidence that they would receive a supportive response from social services, they nevertheless were in no doubt that they had to bring their concerns to the authorities' attention.

The mother of a six-year-old girl who was abused by her stepfather comments:

> I didn't feel that the social worker was very sympathetic. She did not explain very clearly why she needed to know certain things and what would happen. She kept questioning me about why I did not know something was going on – as if I had not asked myself that many times. There was always a veiled threat in the way she dealt with me....All the time it felt very much that if I did not do as they (social services) suggested then my daughter would be taken away. Her attitude towards me was like I must have known what was going on but turned a blind eye towards it. That was very difficult for me to deal with, especially when it was me that initially went to them (social services) for help in the first place.

It is pertinent to consider the effects of the child protection process on mothers and their families. The intrusive nature of child protection work engenders powerlessness in mothers. The tensions that are generated for mothers are compounded by the ideas they may hold (real or perceived) about the negative nature of statutory agencies' responses. It is certainly the case that marginalised groups often have the most to fear about how others will see their parenting. Let us not forget that black parents' childrearing and caregiving are held to a different standard, and essentially differing assumptions about roles and responsibilities means it is mothers who become the targets of surveillance.

This mother describes how she experienced the intervention of social services:

> You become very conscious of your role, your limitations and the power of professionals. I felt that the social worker had a condescending attitude towards me...and did not understand, or could imagine what I was going through....I felt I just had to leave it up to them (social workers). I had dealings with social services in the past when my son was excluded from school and started to get involved in petty crime, so I know from first hand experience how they can make you feel – that you are failing as a mother. It made me very angry.

For those families where a full child protection investigation took place, the effects of the process on mothers and their families were to leave them feeling disempowered and estranged from each other. It is fundamentally those mothers who felt disempowered by the investigative processes that reported not feeling helped by statutory agencies' intervention. For some, the effects of the investigative process left them feeling devalued and blamed. Some mothers reported that they were thus mistrustful of professionals and did not want to divulge details of their intimate lives that show that things were not working in their families. Typically, mothers described that once the initial child protection investigation was over, they were left with little or no family support services, or therapeutic input to help deal with the effects of their children's abuse. Some of these mothers had to rely on supportive networks of families and friends to manage in the aftermath of the abuse, whilst others struggled on their own. The findings from this research add strength to the argument that mothers are often left unsupported to deal with children's behavioural problems as well as the effects of the abuse on other family members (Family Rights Group, 1996; Farmer and Owen, 1995; Gibbons, Conroy and Bell, 1995; Jackson and Tuscon, 1999). For example, in their study of the child protection system of two local authorities, Farmer and Owen noted that the initial impact of investigation is traumatic, alienating and disempowering for families. The thrust of the intervention with families is on investigation, and few families received therapeutic input, nor were they provided with the family support services that are essential in the aftermath of sexual abuse. The point being stressed is that the needs of children's significant carers, their mothers, were addressed in only a small number of cases. It is thought that whilst

83

this might be linked to professionals' concern to maintain a focus on the safety needs of children; nevertheless the needs of children cannot be fully addressed without considering the factors that impact their mothers' ability to protect them from harm (Mittler, 1997).

Mothers' Perception of the Helping Process

In contrast, a number of mothers had not involved child protection services. As highlighted previously, the findings revealed that this was more likely to happen where the abuser was the woman's husband or male partner, or someone else close to the family.

For example, one mother explains her reasons for not involving social services when her nine-year-old daughter was abused by her partner (not the child's father):

> In the days after I found out, I thought I was going nutty. You know, I really felt like I was from Mars or something. At that stage, I didn't think I could go to any professionals or they would lock me up. And yet, my decision not to go to the professionals was also influenced in part by discussions with my daughter as well. I didn't want to put her through any more stress, and to be honest I was fearful of what may happen to my daughter.

This mother may indeed have believed she was protecting her daughter by not subjecting her to what she perceived will be a stigmatising intervention from the child protection services. There is, however, an uneasy position to grapple with, namely that some mothers' decisions may indeed unwittingly leave some black children exposed to further harm. Given this dilemma, a key concern is that while some mothers' family networks and support systems may offer protection to children, others may not. Particularly when the abuse is intrafamilial, some families may compound children's difficulties, by perpetuating the silence, denial and secrecy that normally surround child sexual abuse. Therefore, there may be a tension here between the interests of mothers, their children's needs, an extended families wish not to have family business discussed outside the home.

One of the main reasons mothers gave for not approaching social services departments was perceived racism and discrimination within the institutional structures of statutory agencies. For some mothers, their concern for the racism that their children may encounter was a significant factor in influencing their choices. Some mothers expressed feelings of deep mistrust of professionals and invariably feared that their children would be removed from them. Additionally, some black mothers may not necessarily see professionals as protectors of their communities, but may indeed see them as part of the problem. For example, Farmer and Owen (1996) noted that black families were particularly disadvantaged in relation to service provision by not being provided with an appropriate worker who understands their needs. Consequently, some mothers may indeed see themselves as protecting their children by not subjecting them to what they perceive to be coercive intervention from statutory agencies.

Understandably, black mothers clearly feel they have to weigh up not only how to seek help, but also to be selective about whom they approach, because of fear of further stigmatisation and a negative reaction. Additionally, some do not want to betray their families. Foremost in the minds of a number of the mothers was that they might experience a negative result as a consequence of accessing formal helping services. What was also at stake for some mothers is that the consequences of involving the police could be marginalisation or exclusion from their communities (Bernard, 1997). These factors will significantly influence black mothers' decisions about using child protection services or law enforcement agencies as a solution for dealing with the aftermath child sexual abuse. As I indicated earlier, although some mothers reported feeling betrayed and angry on discovery of the abuse, they still wished to protect their partners from punitive intervention and so were reluctant to seek the support of professional helpers or law enforcement agencies. Arguably, intervention with mothers that is not underpinned with a clear analysis of how gender and race inscribe their perception of the helping process runs the risk of being oppressive and will influence the likely outcomes for their children.

However, not all experiences of the helping process were negative. The findings also revealed examples of mothers viewing the help they received from social services in a very positive light. Some mothers reported being very satisfied with the input from professionals and they especially valued efforts to involve them in decision-making, without judging their actions.

The mother of a nine-year-old girl who was abused by a close family friend offers some reflections on the help she received from her social worker:

The female social worker that they allocated to me gave me strength, talking me through the issues. She made me realise it wasn't my fault, I had no control over it happening....That helped a lot for me to put some things into perspective and not feel a sense of failure because my daughter's name was put on the child protection register.

What appeared to make a difference for this mother was that she felt heard and not blamed throughout the child protection investigative process. This mother clearly valued the efforts of the social worker to be open, honest, and clear with her about the purpose of intervention, how and why certain decisions would be made, what was expected of her and importantly, what demands would be made of her. For this mother, that the social worker provided clear boundaries and created space for her to examine her options in a non-blaming environment helped to make the intervention an empowering one. She described valuing the efforts to involve her as much as was possible in the decision-making processes as well as providing her with the support that was necessary for her to enhance her parenting of her daughter. For example, this mother's had participated in a group for carers of children who had been sexually abused, whilst her daughter had received some therapeutic input.

Similarly, another mother whose eleven-year-old daughter was abused by her stepfather describes how aspect of social work intervention helped:

After the investigation and case conference was over the social worker referred me to a group for mothers of children who had been sexually abused. At first I was very nervous about attending a group, but I am now glad that I did. It provided me with a good support network and gave me encouragement. Before going to the group I had become very withdrawn because I found it really difficult to talk to anyone – my extended family or friends. I thought they would not understand and I suppose to a certain extent, I thought they would blame me. I couldn't find the words, you know....I became isolated and was very depressed and not coping very well at all. The most helpful thing about the group was that I had other mothers to share my story with who understood what I was going through and I was able to learn how not to blame myself and deal with the feelings of guilt that I felt. Sharing my experiences with other mothers who had been through a similar experience has helped me realise that I'm not the only one this has happened to. The group has helped me to understand my daughter's needs better – you know not take it so much as a personal failure as a mother that I did not know what was going on. I was also able to get ideas to help me to deal with some of my daughter's behaviour, which at times is difficult to cope with. There are days when it feels as if

I'm still living in a nightmare, but attending the group has made me a much more confident person and it is really helping me to strengthen my relationship with my daughter.

This mother was clearly able to identify the benefits of the group work for her, and her story illustrates most powerfully that having others who have been through a similar experience to talk to can mediate the stressors brought about by the abuse. Importantly, she was able to articulate some of the insights and awareness she had gained from participating in the group to consider how it is helping her daughter.

Discussion

Exploring black mothers' help-seeking behaviour in the aftermath of abuse raises important questions about risk estimation for children's safety and developmental needs. An important message emerging from this study is the significance of the mothers' own agency and action in protecting their children from further harm. It has been suggested that given the complexity of feelings mothers experience, many may feel uncertain in the routes open to them to seek help. They are also presented with a number of difficulties to meet their children's emotional and developmental needs. The findings suggest that some mothers had to demonstrate great resilience in coping with obstacles to get help for their children. Important glimpses are offered into the struggles for mothers in trying to take action on their children's behalf. Effectively, what point of reference mothers begin from to interpret and make sense of their children's safety needs will be significantly influenced by the internal narratives and external constraints on them. Certainly, it is by considering the ways in which mothers articulate their parenting needs in the aftermath of abuse that it becomes possible to identify the particular ways in which the risk factors for their children are compounded. It is probably true to say that in spite of many mothers' best efforts, some children's needs will nevertheless go unmet. Unquestionably, it seems unlikely that risks for children would be reduced if mothers' parenting was not strengthened. In many ways, some mothers may have the personal capacity to respond in an emotionally supportive manner to their children, but they may not have had the opportunities to explore the strengths and difficulties in their parenting in a non-blaming environment; for considering what they have to do to improve their ability to offer "reasonable parental care" to ensure that their children are effectively protected from further harm (DOH, 1989; Erooga and Print, 2000).

Most specifically, in establishing thresholds for intervention, particular challenges are posed for practitioners in how they manage the tensions inherent in working with difference structured around race and its implications for defining the threshold criteria for intervening in black families. A central concern for practitioners is that race and gender are critically important areas for considering their impact on the construction of risk and defining thresholds for intervention. For example, without an examination of the assumptions, values, and attitudes they hold about black families in general, and black mothers in particular, the caregiving provided in these families will be differentially valued and evaluated, resulting in a conception of harm that may establish lower or higher thresholds for intervention. Ultimately, conscious or unconscious assumptions about abuse in black families – the reliance on cultural stereotyping – could unwittingly lead to the acceptance of different expectations for black children, thus compromising their safety needs. Although the child protection mandate under section 47 of the Children Act (1989) gives professionals a duty to intervene in families to protect children following allegations of child sexual abuse, no clear definition of abuse is provided in the guidance to establish levels of harm. In one sense, this lack of specification of harm has a number of significant implications for defining thresholds of intervention with black families. An important consideration is that considerable discretion is left to practitioners and managers' professional decision-making processes to judge the probability and likelihood of harm within the broad framework of the Children Act. Consequently, it could be argued that as soon as practitioners hit the threshold for intervention with black families a range of factors, such as personal and organisational values, resources and ideologies determine the way in which practitioners and their managers interpret and define harm and perceptions of risk (Banks, 2000; Chand, 2000). Furthermore, the implicitly racialised assumptions that can manifest itself in overt and covert ways to shape the experience of black families in the child protection system need to be uncovered (Boushel, 2000). Most definitely, for the needs of black children to be effectively addressed, attention needs to be paid to the dynamics that may be embedded in child protection discourse and practice with black families in general, and black mothers in particular, that can play an important role in lowering or increasing levels of intervention for black children.

Accordingly, the identification of risk situations for black children requires consideration to be given to a diverse array of factors in a systematic way. Specifically, identifying and assessing risk demands the gathering of a wide range of evidence (Corby, 1998; Munro, 1998). Moreover, some of the methods that need to be utilised for assessing long-term risk involves working with parents over a long period to assess their potential for becoming safe parents (Corby, 1996). Thus, as has been noted: "protecting the interests of black children may well involve the intensive supervision of their parents" (Channer and Parton, 1988, p.105). This begs the question, what are the implications of the social policing role of such an approach for practice with black mothers, as it is their parenting that will come up for close scrutiny in any assessment processes. In fact, one might argue that a key factor in establishing thresholds of intervention rests largely on the appraisal of mothers' parenting. Such an analysis points to the fundamental importance of not only understanding the ways race will powerfully influence how black children give voice to their experiences, and how mothers access support to deal with the consequences of abuse, but most crucially, race is also a defining feature in how practitioners develop estimation of risk for black children. A major challenge, therefore, lies in asking the difficult and complex questions about the impact of race and gender in shaping choices, helping-seeking and help-giving (Banks, 2000; Maitra, 1995; Thanki, 1994). More precisely, when risk analysis is grounded in an understanding of gendered power relations in black families, intervention can build effectively on black mothers' protective strategies, thus ensuring their children are not left exposed to further harm.

Clearly, creating an environment where resistant mothers and avoidant fathers can be engaged with, whilst maintaining a clear focus on children's needs, is not easy and will require the adoption of multiple modes of intervention; for example, direct work with children, work with parents together and separately where relevant. Most powerfully, the challenges in keeping children's safety needs as paramount whilst striving to achieve partnership with parents will be anxiety-provoking, and practitioners will struggle to stay with the guiding principles of the Children Act; notably, working in partnership. Whilst working in partnership does not always mean agreeing with mothers, it is essential that they understand the processes and the purpose of child protection involvement at each stage of the intervention (DOH, 1995; Thoburn, Lewis, and Shemmings, 1995). The underlying difficulty for practitioners is how to affirm the strengths and resilience of non-abusing black mothers, whilst not avoiding the critical interrogation of the ways in which their behaviours may create risk situations for their children. For instance, in carrying out core assessments, a deeper and more careful consideration of the main factors that affect black mothers' parenting circumstances is essential if practitioners are to accurately assess why some mothers may fall short in providing reasonable parental care in the aftermath of abuse. Notably, a deeper understanding of black mothers' strengths and limitations enhances the possibilities of practitioners being able to see them as effective allies in the protection of their children. Ultimately, intervention that facilitates mothers using their own strengths and experiences to find solutions to their situations is potentially more empowering for them and their children.

In sum, the findings confirm the importance of recognising that supported mothers are often in a very strong position to offer support and protection, and also to help their children in their struggles to develop and maintain a positive sense of self in the aftermath of victimisation. Unfortunately, the findings illuminate that these mothers were often left alone to deal with the behavioural and emotional disorders that their children developed in the aftermath of sexual abuse. Given the salience of the issues facing black mothers, how practitioners build on their strengths and strategies to protect their children is of critical importance. This point is pertinent because it essentially opens up a space to consider the pivotal role mothers can play in the recovery process for their children (Hooper, 1992; Walton, 1999). Above all, the support that mothers are given can hinder or strengthen their parenting. Without some examination of the contradictions and conflicts facing black mothers, some professionals may intervene in ways that are insensitive, coercive, and punitive (Bernard, 1997).

7 Conclusion: Ways Forward for Practice Intervention with Black Families

This book has been centrally about addressing connections between race and gender in framing black mothers' emotional and behavioural responses to the sexual abuse of their children. In particular, the findings from the research that forms the basis of this book chart the ways that women's mothering roles are impacted in the aftermath of abuse. Thus, this book has sought to help illuminate some of the complex relationships that are contributory factors in shaping the concrete circumstances of women's mothering. In weaving together the voices of mothers with an analysis that draws largely on insights derived from anti-racist and black feminist thinking, I have attempted to develop a paradigm that is grounded in an understanding of gendered power relations within black families, to elucidate the implications for black mothers' parenting of their sexually abused children.

From the analysis provided in preceding chapters, several issues are explicated. For instance, the complex situations many black mothers confront were most clearly illustrated by the number that experienced conflictual feelings. Additionally, divided loyalties presented serious dilemmas for mothers. Notably, these elements are particularly illustrative of the practical and emotional constraints on mothers, essentially affecting their efforts to help their children deal with the traumatising impact of the abuse. As has been indicated, mothers' responses are characterised by a profound ambivalence and there are deep tensions at the intersection of race and gender. Arguably, the shame, despair and humiliation mothers suffer play a powerful role in influencing how they negotiate the contradictory demands to meet their children's needs. In this final chapter, I briefly sketch out some key considerations that are essential for guiding policy and practice initiatives for social work intervention with black families.

Assessment of Parenting in the Aftermath of Abuse

Black women's mothering remains central to risk analysis for their children, as they inevitably continue to bear the prime responsibility for caregiving in families and it is them whom children largely depend on for care and protection. It is increasingly acknowledged that empowered mothers can provide a valuable and potentially unique contribution to the different stages of their children's recovery (Hooper and Humphreys, 1998; Skinner, 2000). However, as I have highlighted, black mothers have additional problems to overcome as they struggle to support their children through the recovery process. Essentially, on discovery of abuse, black mothers face the complicated task of having to negotiate a path through what are often unsupportive and even at times outright hostile environments, from a position of being socially powerless, to get support and justice for their children. These are compounding factors in mothers' help-seeking and bring about a hesitation to access statutory services; a hesitation that is likely to be rooted in years of bad experiences (Ahmed, 1988).

In particular, in the aftermath of abuse black mothers' caregiving and parenting is subjected to an intense scrutiny. It might be supposed that in a context where black women's experiences are rendered invisible or conversely marginalised, the criterion for assessing their mothering practices will be seen through a racialised lens that results in their experiences being evaluated differently. To be sure, these are crucial elements for making evaluative judgements about the parenting practices provided by black mothers. Indeed, practitioners might implicitly assess black women's mothering practices in terms of how well their parenting conforms to white middle-class ideals. Also, preconceived ideas professional helpers may hold about what makes a good mother may make it more likely that black mothers, who already carry a devalued status, are most often seen as dysfunctional and unstable (Bryan, 1992). Certainly, making judgements about "good-enough" mothering is a complex and multi-layered process that is saturated with gendered, racialised, and class assumptions. Whilst it could be argued that constructions of good and bad mothering function to make all mothers vulnerable to mother-blaming in child welfare and protection paradigms, these ideas have particular resonance for black mothers because their parenting practices are devalued to start with. Viewed thus, one might expect that black mothers would have a hard time "measuring up" to the good mother image. Indeed, in a climate that routinely portrays black parents as deficit, some black mothers' perceptions are that Eurocentric assumptions about "good-enough" parenting increases the likelihood that they will experience a negative intervention from the helping authorities. My data showed that these perceptions had undoubtedly influenced some mothers to be disinclined to involve professional helpers on discovery of abuse. Another interesting finding of the research is the extent to which the negative portrayal of black families consciously and unconsciously influenced some mothers' decisions whether and how to involve formal helping services. It is especially important to understand the ways in which deep-rooted attitudes and beliefs influence and distort black mothers' everyday realities, affecting their perceptions and thus making them mistrustful of professional helpers.

To appreciate the challenges facing black mothers necessitates recognising that at the heart of their experiences are the way relations of domination and subordination in their network of family relationships operates to create a context where they are beset with conflict-ridden situations. Unquestionably, the complex power relations embodied in black families give rise to a set of circumstances, which means black mothers are often caught between their own needs and wishes, and the expectations of families and partners that they be loyal. Importantly, these elements need to be unravelled for understanding the conditions that lead to conflicting loyalties that ultimately have implications for women's parenting. An exploration of these factors provides additional insights into why some mothers may not voluntarily involve child protection services on discovery of abuse. Therefore, in considering methods of intervention to foster alliances with black mothers, practice must be grounded in knowledge of how matrixes of domination compound mothers' difficult experiences. There are also other implications. Perhaps the devaluation of black women's mothering inhibits the possibilities for identifying their complicated coping mechanisms and limits us from understanding how they pursue their options. It is undeniable that professional helpers starting from a deficit perspective will fail to recognise the ways that mothers' parenting practices accentuate some of their protective mechanisms. Rather than focus solely on the deficits in black mothers' parenting, practitioners also need to explore the complexities facing them in order to enhance intervention for working from a strengths' perspective to form an alliance for the protection of black children.

Involving Black Fathers and Father-figures

The issues involved for mothers are further complicated by how practitioners involve and work with black men in the family. For example,

93

in chapter five I point to the ways a number of mothers were in relationships with men who were not the children's biological fathers, did not have parental responsibility for their children, and who were not actively involved in their children's lives, but nonetheless spent a good deal of time in their households. Mothers' capacity to provide "good-enough" parenting in this context is crucially linked to the nature and quality of her relationship with the perpetrator and this is especially what can create contradictory understandings. In such circumstances, some women felt guilty that their children did not have a "proper" father around. Moreover, this set of dynamics will frame the quality and nature of mothers' relationship with their children; significantly impacting on their abilities to ensure that their children's best interests remains at the centre of their decision-making. It is this nexus that we need to look closely at to understand what is happening in a family for identifying high-risk situations for black children. The cumulative effects of abuse in these types of alternative family structures mean that there can be a source of strain on children and their needs and anxieties could easily be overlooked as mothers struggle to maintain a sense of self and any semblance of coping. More specifically, consideration of these issues alerts us to the kinds of questions that we need to think about in making assessment of risk that does not rest entirely on mother-blaming beliefs. It will seriously exercise practitioners to understand the set of dynamics that are posed and the impact on children's emotional well-being, and perhaps most crucially, women's capacity to parent competently. In making assessments of risks in such situations, there is a danger that men's presence will remain invisible as little attempt is made to assess the significance of their involvement with these families and to focus exclusively on mothers. The main point I mean to stress, however, is that circumstances like these will provide many challenges for practitioners in how they hold these men accountable and involve them in any assessment of risk for children.

A number of authors have commented on the reluctance of practitioners generally to draw invisible men into child protection systems (Milner, 1993; Milner, 1996; O'Hagan and Dillenburger, 1995; Trotter, 1997). In her analysis of the differing career paths of fathers and mothers in child protection, Milner calls attention to the ways stereotypical ideas of black fathers were drawn upon to make assertions about their supposed lack of involvement in the caregiving of their children. Crucially, prevailing assumptions reflect a widespread belief about the supposed "dangerousness", "fecklessness" and "irresponsibility" of black men that may implicitly inform practitioners' decisions not to strenuously involve black fathers or father-figures, and thus promote a negative attention on mothers. To this end, whilst we need to understand the wider context of the black male experience in Britain, we also need to find ways to do so without excusing black men's abuse against the women and children in their lives, thus making visible the factors that encourages and support silence about male violence in the home. It is important to keep in mind that whilst some dimensions of racist assumptions that permeate child welfare provision affect black mothers and fathers in similar ways, the gender specific mechanism of racism affects them in quite distinct ways (Carby, 1992). So essentially, it is mothers and not fathers that are held to a higher standard around notions of "good enough" parenting, which means regardless of who the abuser is, mothers are always deeply implicated in the abuse of their children. Moreover, a reliance on stereotypical ideas can lead to over-looking gender inequalities in black families and perhaps more importantly, abuse can be explained away on cultural grounds (i.e. it is normal behaviour in black families) therefore essentially leaving black children exposed to further harm. Ultimately, the assumptions and ideas that practitioners draw upon to underscore their professional judgements will be predicated on cultural and racial stereotypes of black men, women and families. Practitioners who do not confront theses issues in work with black families and base their intervention on assumptions about the nature of male-female relationships in black families are unwittingly colluding with gender inequalities, and will loose sight of how their intervention will replay or reproduce dominant power relationships in these families. By centrally addressing gender and race as a locus of power relations, we can begin to delineate the specificities around parenting roles and responsibilities in black families to make distinctions between abusing and non-abusing black parents. Fundamentally, policy and practice initiatives underpinned by the philosophy of "invisible fathers" serve to perpetuate the idea that it is the mother's sole responsibility to protect children and fundamentally reinforce mother-blaming. In this regard, how welfare policies and practice formulate parenting roles is of critical importance.

Balancing the Needs and Rights of Black Children against those of their Mothers

Practitioners have to strike a difficult balance between the protection of black children and the rights and responsibilities of their parents. The main challenge for practitioners is to be able to weigh up the risks for children, whilst at the same time work in an enabling an empowering way with their primary carers. Of importance is the need to identify and work from a strengths' perspective with black mothers, whilst simultaneously working with fathers, father-figures or other significant others involved in children's lives. Primarily, starting from a strengths' approach with black mothers acknowledges those characteristics that enabled or hindered some in seeking help and support to parent their children in the aftermath of abuse. Understanding the key dynamics for mothers – their relationship with the child's abuser; the grieving process for mothers – as sources of stress and barriers to affecting change, will illuminate understandings of the risk factors for children. Nevertheless, identifying and working with the strengths of black mothers in the context of risk is problematic and ultimately children's safety needs could be compromised. Though practitioners need to take on board the barriers for black mothers in being able to secure their children's safety, they also have to be vigilant not to conflate children's and mothers' needs. Clearly, it will challenge practitioners in their endeavours to explore the inherent tensions in order to identify when mothers' and children's needs may be enmeshed. Notwithstanding, the rights of children to have their needs evaluated independently from their mothers are the over-riding concern. Practitioners are thus charged with assisting black mothers to create a different frame of reference to help them understand their own needs but also at the same time enable them to make changes to meet the needs of their children.

Some Practice Implications

In this book, I have attempted to show that to effectively assess the needs of black mothers and their children points the way toward making connections with different forms of oppression to fully comprehend the stresses and uncertainties that the discovery of abuse brings for mothers. Some key issues that have arisen from this research have been around questions of empowerment, and the best ways of delivering a service that meets the needs of black children and their families. A number of implications for policy and practice have thus been raised. Most significantly, we must generally re-think our approach to black mothers in child protection work. Above all, given the significance of the issues confronting black mothers, one of the key tasks of helping professionals must always be to question, acknowledge and confront mothers' lived realities to understand their motivations and coping processes (Williams, 1999). Essentially, understanding the processes that underlie black mothers' parenting requires an examination of how power relations in their families operate to create a context where they are beset with conflict-ridden situations. This argument stems from the view that formulating black mothers' responses as experiences grounded in their social realities helps us to recognise the relationships of power in their lives for discerning their coping behaviours and help-seeking efforts in the aftermath of abuse. Importantly, the contradictory elements of mothers' experiences need to be unravelled for making sense of the conditions for women that lead to having conflicting loyalties that impact their parenting capacity.

I have illustrated throughout this book some of the ways black mothers perceived and experienced the helping process. It is evident that some mothers may not find their encounters with professional helpers to be comfortable exchanges. Indeed, as 1 indicated in chapter six some mothers experienced child protection services as a hostile and alien environment and these mothers particularly feared encountering racism. Mothers essentially require a safe and supportive space to explore the complexities inherent in their situations, and to make sense of and communicate their own experiences without fear of being judged harshly. Importantly, mothers' feelings of anger and uncertainties will need to be expressed away from accusations of complicity. As I highlighted in chapter six a number of mothers in the study who utilised the help of social services cited the efforts by practitioners to be clear with them about what the concerns were and also what their expectations were of them as being especially helpful. Unquestionably, openness is an important feature of the support that professional helpers need to offer mothers. Professionals need to develop ways of empowering family members by being clear with them about what is and is not negotiable (Mittler, 1997). This starting point increases the possibility that professional helpers would be enabled in their tasks to assist mothers' parenting for providing appropriate responses to their children.

One means of supporting mothers is to identify and draw on the positive coping strategies that they employ. As we saw in chapter five, some mothers were able to utilise supportive kinship networks that gave care and support to help protect their children. Supportive family members were also mobilised by mothers as a valuable resource, for example, to confront abusive men. The crucial issue for mothers is that being able to take control is a powerful act that enables them to foster alliances with their children. Good support is a key to resilience and it was especially those mothers who were isolated that struggled most with conflictual emotions and ambivalent responses to their children. Practitioners need to understand what this process involves for mothers in order to recognise the difficulties they are experiencing, so as to build on their strengths in order to boost their efforts to protect their children. It is precisely because isolation is a key vulnerability factor – not only for mothers, but also more importantly for the children involved – that practitioners need to understand how isolation can compound risk for black children.

Practitioners can ultimately play a critical role in assisting mothers to make sense of some of their ambivalent feelings and conflictual emotions, and to understand the impact of their behaviour on their children. Hence, to allow work to carry out that utilises mothers' resiliency frameworks, how mothers' efforts to support their children are validated is of significance. Thus, professional helpers are in a powerful position to bring about positive change, or conversely to compound the difficulties black mothers encounter. To assist mothers to carry out their parenting role, interventions that will help to make a difference to children are the kind that are able to garner the strengths of mothers, and validate the resources which mothers mobilised in their own, and their children's interest as routes out of abusive relationships. In this sense, helpful intervention is one that comes with a grounded insight into mothers' situations and has at its core knowledge of their lived experiences so as not to obscure the real problems they face.

To enhance mothers' potential for ensuring their children's interests are not compromised, anti-oppressive values and ideas must be at the heart of interventions with black families. Essentially, to engage effectively with black mothers, professional helpers need to draw on anti-oppressive frameworks in order to understand how mothers' gendered and racialised locations impact on their parenting at this critical time. As I have highlighted throughout, race will not only influence attitudes towards black mothers, but will also profoundly frame how they perceive their choices and help-seeking patterns in the aftermath of the abuse. Grasping the significance of these factors is vital if practice is to build on mothers' coping and resilience mechanisms. Professional responsibility and authority is central to the decision-making processes of child protection work and how practitioners' own power bases structured around their gender, race, class, and authority position, will profoundly influence the assessment process (Munro, 1998). Indeed, there are some specific issues involved for practitioners – of same or different racial backgrounds to mothers – which need to be drawn out for considering the implications for anti-oppressive practice.

For example, white practitioners working with the differences structured around race may experience anxieties about whether racial stereotyping might be informing their interventions with black families (Dominelli, 1988). These practitioners may fear that their intervention will be interpreted as racist. Thus may be hindered in their ability to ask some of the necessary difficult questions and to confront mothers where they need to, as well as hold the men involved accountable in order to make assessments that do not blame mothers nor impede the interests of children. Moreover, some may be so cautious in their intervention that they may fail to intervene with the professional authority that their statutory powers grant them, and their inaction can leave black children exposed to further harm. Important to note that a number of child abuse inquiries into the deaths of black children, such as, Tyra Henry and Sukina Hammond, have highlighted a lack of intervention is situations where these children were at obvious risk of suffering harm from their parents (HMSO, 2000). Mostly, the anxieties experienced by white practitioners to avoid a charge of racism can impede them from intervening in black families and immobilise attempts to move forward. Conversely, without some examination of the values and ideas that they bring to the work, some white practitioners may intervene in ways that are insensitive and heavy-handed thus reinforcing mother-blaming and stereotyping (Bernard, 1997).

On the other hand, black practitioners are faced with a different set of issues around race. It cannot be assumed that similarities around race and gender will automatically mean the interventions will be less problematic. As I have argued elsewhere, though black practitioners may be more likely to adopt an anti-racist approach in their work with mothers, some may draw exclusively on race as a framework of analysis, and ignore or gloss over the significance of gendered power relationship in mediating black mothers' experiences in families (Bernard, 2000). Furthermore, black practitioners occupational situatedness may mean they do not have decision-making powers due to their subordinate status in their organisations (Lewis, 1996). As a consequence, they may be constrained in their abilities to translate their commitment to anti-oppressive values into practice. Clearly, all practitioners have to pay attention to the importance of race and racism in shaping definitions of harm and perceptions of risk (Ahmad, 1989; Humphreys, Atkar and Baldwin, 1999; Maitra, 1995). Nevertheless a focus solely on race and cultural factors leaves unquestioned issues of gender oppression and power relationships that are inevitably embedded in black mothers' experiences. For effective work with black families to take place, practitioners of all racial backgrounds must recognise the need for reflexivity in order to be constantly attuned to the way their values, situated experiences, and perspectives shape their interventions if they are to avoid an oppressive practice with black mothers.

Fundamentally, without re-inscribing racism, professional helpers need to be able to question mothers' motivations and actions without devaluing their strategies for coping from their own experiences. More specifically, it is by being observant of mothers' perspectives that we can begin to develop anti-oppressive interventions that facilitate the assessments of parenting that are critical, particularly where non-abusing mothers can be seen as allies in the safety planning for their children. Best

99

practice in working with mothers and their families requires involving mothers actively in the decision-making processes. This is a step towards anti-oppressive practice for it would not only help to reduce the tendency to blame mothers, but would also enable them to participate fully in any Section 47 child protection investigations.

Above all, to assess and build on the positive value of mothers' contribution to their children's recovery requires critical reflective professionals who have the analytic capacities necessary for explicating the pertinent issues, whilst at the same time managing high levels of uncertainties. It is not uncommon for child protection workers to be overwhelmed in working with families where child sexual abuse has occurred. Moreover, there are multiple interpretations of mothers' roles and sometimes the understandings are diametrically opposed, so that it makes it difficult to have any certainty. Child protection work is an area where uncertainties, confusion, controversy and contradictions assail; and practitioners are involved in making complex value assessments of risk in a context of competing truths, constraints and pressures, and especially in a climate of blame; whilst at the same time having to manage the anxieties that this can provoke (Parton, 1996; Cooper, 2000). Making estimations of risk, and risk management in conflict-ridden situation, are at the heart of child protection work (Bagley, 1999). Inevitably, practitioners will be seriously exercised in their attempts to work with the strengths of black mothers and delineate the dilemmas and contradictions they will be faced with from an anti-oppressive stance. This necessitates practitioners having the skill to manage high levels of ambiguity, but most critically they also require a supportive management culture for managing the inherent uncertainties that this work entails. Parton's analysis provides valuable insights into the debates of risk in the empirical and theoretical literature on child protection, and in particular, has highlighted the way constructions about risks encourage a reliance on predictive factors and a checklist approach to making assessments. Most notably, the reliance on predictive factors and checklists as tools to evaluate risk encourages a striving for certainty in a very uncertain field, thus obscuring a very complex process involving power relationships (Parton, 1998).

How practitioners manage the uncertainties, contradictions, ambiguities, and complexities so inherent in black mothers' situations will depend largely on what knowledge and frameworks they draw on to underpin their interventions. Arguably, a failure to grapple with the uncertainties and complexities can mean that the anxiety which child protection work engenders in practitioners may result in an oppressive intervention with families. This can reject out of hand the necessity to wrestle with the tensions and uncertainties involved in attempting to work in an empowering way with black families. There are, off course, a range of factors that would influence practitioners' willingness and capacity to struggle with the uncertainties. Most notably, for the majority of front-line practitioners and their managers there is the very real fear that should something go wrong, they will be subject to a Public Inquiry (Parton, 1997). In the majority of cases social workers bear the brunt of criticism when things go wrong in child abuse cases. Ultimately, however, practitioners should not uncritically accept an interpretation of risk that pays little attention to the broader social and political context in which black mothers' parenting are constructed.

A key argument of this book has been that there is not a shared understanding of mothers' responses. It particularly seeks to alert us to the fact that mothers of abused children are not all coming from the same starting point and calls attention to the complexity and diversity of their experiences. It is evident that black mothers cannot simply be added on to existing theories, but need to be at the core of the analysis to illuminate the ways assumptions stemming from racialised differentiated representations of gender influence appraisal of their parenting capacity (Carby, 1992). As such, this book does not seek to provide the definitive account of black mothers' positions. I offer this analysis instead as alternative ways of conceptualising black mothers' experiences and the problems that arise for them in parenting their children in the aftermath of abuse. Essentially, this investigation directs our gaze to the complexities that have to be unravelled to make visible the hidden, most notably how the subtle and pervasive processes of the twin obstacles for mothers, race and gender oppression, intertwine to create the contradictory demands that are placed on them. The value of this analysis is that it draws our attention to the multi-faceted nature of black mothers' circumstances and provides us with a means for interrogating the complications inherent for them. Moreover, this analysis is important for bringing into full view the varying layers of black mothers' lived realities to dispel some of the misconceptions that exist about collusive mothers. I have argued throughout that a narrow conception of mothers' collusion fails to shed light on the multiplicity of factors that pose a challenge to black mothers' ability to ensure that the interests of their children remain paramount. Especially important is the need to develop frameworks to conceptualise mothers' experiences by forcefully challenging the prevailing assumptions that customarily characterise them as complicit. Thus, the standpoint expounded herein moves away from explanations of women's actions as collusive to one that is underpinned with knowledge of how gender and race inscribe black mothers' parenting.

There is a need for existing policy and practice frameworks to be refrained and broadened if they are to be valuable for guiding interventions with black families. The inquiry provided in this book offers a useful starting point for locating black mothers' experiences to illuminate the barriers to them accessing help that meet theirs and their children's needs. Policy initiatives developed from research founded on the experiences of black mothers will be better able to bring an understanding of how their mothering experiences are distinct in a number of significant ways to consider the many implications for practice interventions. Given that crucial dimensions of mothers' experiences are hidden, the usefulness of this research is the opportunity it affords some mothers to articulate their concerns so that their voices can be brought more centrally into the public domain. Essentially, users of research; practitioners, policy makers, and service providers, need to hear the testimonies of black mothers so that their experiences can be part of the agenda on debates about child welfare and protection. Certainly, hearing from black mothers directly provides valuable insights into their perspectives to appreciate the challenges for them in parenting their sexually victimised children. At the risk of stating the obvious, we need to be able to hear from mothers themselves about their understandings of their children's needs; for we will not value their protective strategies, and most importantly, we will not understand from their point of view the factors that may act as obstacles to effective parenting for promoting the best interests of their children. In essence, by grounding practice in an understanding of the significance of race and gender as important categories of experience, we can provide a critical framework for assessing the complexity for black mothers in the aftermath of abuse.

In sum, perhaps a key message from this research is that as black mothers experience complex layers of oppression, ways of understanding the broader social forces that shape their lived realities are necessary to be aware of the challenges they face in ensuring that their children are not left in harmful situations. Undoubtedly, the failure of professional helpers to rigorously grapple with complex power relationships involved in childhood sexual abuse in black families compounds victims' psychological distress, and amplifies mothers' feelings of self-blame, thus reinforcing the silence and secrecy on which abuse depends (Bernard, 1997). The fact remains, however, that mothers will continue to be the key figures in the maintenance of their children's welfare. As this and other research has revealed, a well-supported mother is an important source of protection for children. The empowered mother has a lot to offer her abused child. Thus, it is proposed that one of the best ways to ensure that abused black children's psychic and emotional well-being remains at the centre of practice intervention is to shore up their mothers' parenting by providing them with the right kind of support and resources necessary for effectively safeguarding their children's welfare and development. Professional helpers who fail to get hold of these ideas run the risk of undermining mothers' contribution to this process because they may not attach enough importance to the protective and coping strategies of black mothers and will ultimately' assess their capacity for adaptation and change from a deficit standpoint. Practitioners who overemphasise a deficit model of parenting and de-emphasise the concrete life experiences of mothers run the risk of undermining the potential contribution they can make to the recovery process for their children. Underpinning practice with sound knowledge of the structural, cultural, and emotional processes that underlie mothers' caregiving in the aftermath of abuse will provide an important starting point for optimising mothers' parenting capacities. In arguing that children's recovery from sexual abuse can be facilitated by good support from their mothers, I am making a claim that work with black mothers must be undertaken as part of a larger effort whose ultimate goal is to achieve good outcomes for their children.

Bibliography

Abney, V.D. and Priest, R. (1995), 'African Americans and Sexual Child Abuse', in L.A. Fontes (ed), *Sexual Abuse in Nine North American Cultures: Treatment and Prevention*, Sage, Thousand Oaks, CA, pp.11-30.

Ahmad, B. (1989), 'Protecting Black Children From Abuse', *Social Work Today*, 8 June, p. 24.

Ahmad, B. (1990), *Black Perspectives in Social Work*, Venture Press, Birmingham.

Ahmed, S. (1988), 'Racism in Child Care', in W. Stone and C. Warren (eds), *Protection or Prevention: A Critical Look at the Voluntary Child Care Sector*, NCVCCO, London, pp. 118-124.

Ahmed, T. and Webb-Johnson, A. (1995), 'Voluntary Groups', in S. Fernando (ed), *Mental Health in a Multi-Ethnic Society*, Routledge, London, pp. 74-83.

Alleyne, V. (1997), *There Were Times I Thought I Was Crazy: A Black Woman's Story of Incest*, Sistervision, Toronto.

Andersen, M. L. (1993), 'Studying Across Difference: Race, Class and Gender in Qualitative Research', in J.H.Stanfield II and R.M. Dennis (eds), *Race and Ethnicity in Research Methods*, Sage, Newbury Park, pp. 29-52.

Arshad, R. (1996), 'Building Fragile Bridges: Educating for Change', in K. Cavanagh and V. Cree (eds), *Working With Men: Feminism and Social Work*, Routledge, London, pp. 147-169.

Ashley, S. (1992), *The Missing Voice: Writings by Mothers of Incest Victims*, Kendall/Hunt Publishing Co, Iwoa.

Back, L. (1996), *New Ethnicities and Urban Culture: Racisms and Multiculture in Young Lives*, London, UCL Press.

Back, S. (1998), 'Child Sexual Abuse: Victim Age, Victim Gender, and Observer Gender as Factors Contributing to Attributions of Responsibility', *Child Abuse and Neglect*, Vol.12, No 22, pp. 1239-52.

Bagley, C. (1995), *Child Sexual Abuse and Mental Health in Adolescent and Adults*, Brookfield, VT, Avebury.

Bagley, C. (1999), 'Children First: Challenges and Dilemmas for Social Workers Investigating and Treating Child Sexual Abuse', in C. Bagley and K. Mallick (eds), *Child Sexual Abuse and Adult Offenders: New Theory and Research*, Ashgate, Aldershot, pp. 27-47.

Banks, N. (1999), 'Assessing Risk in Black Families: The Influence of Psychological Dynamics', *Representing Children*, Vol. 12, No 1.

Banks, N. (2000), 'Assessing Children and Families who Belong to Minority Ethnic Groups', in J. Horwath (ed), *The Child's World:Assessing Children in Need*, Department of Health, London, pp. 111-18.

Barn, R. (1993), *Black Children in the Public Care System*, Batsford, London.

Barn, R. (1994a), 'Race and Ethnicity in Social Work: Some Issues for Anti-Discriminatory Research', in B. Humphries and C. Truman (eds), *Re-Thinking Social Research*, Aldershot, Avebury, pp.37-58.

Barn, R. (1994b), 'The Politics of Race Research', *Research Policy and Planning*, Vol. 12, No 2, pp. 13-15.

Barnet, O.W., Miller-Perrin, C.L. and Perrin, R.D. (1997), *Family Violence Across the Lifespan*, Sage, Thousand Oaks, CA.

Baylis, F. and Downie, J. (1997), 'Child Abuse and Neglect: Cross-Cultural Considerations', in H. L. Nelson (ed), *Feminism and Families*, Routledge, London, pp 173-87.

Beddington, A. and Miles, J. (1989), 'The Background of Children who enter Local Authority Care', *British Journal of Social Work*, Vol. 19, pp. 349-68.

Beitchman, J.H., Zucker, K. J., Hood, J. E., DaCosta, G. A., Akman, D. and Cassavia, E. (1992), 'A Review of the Long-term Effects of Child Sexual Abuse', *Child Abuse and Neglect*, Vol. 16, pp. 101-118.

Bell, V. (1993), *Interrogating Incest: Feminist, Foucault and the Law*, Routledge, London.

Bernard, C. (1997), 'Black Mothers' Emotional and Behavioural Responses to the Sexual Abuse of Their Children', in G. Kaufman Kantor and J. L. Jasinski (eds), *Out of the Darkness: Contemporary Perspectives of Family Violence*, Sage, Thousand Oaks, CA, pp. 80-9.

Bernard, C. (1998), 'Race, Gender and Class in Child Sexual Abuse Research', in M. Lavalette, L. Penketh and C. Jones (eds), *Anti-Racism and Social Welfare*, Ashgate, Aldershot, pp.235-54.

Bernard, C. (1999), 'Child Sexual Abuse and the Black Disabled Child', *Disability and Society*, Vol. 14, No 3, pp.325-39.

Bernard, C. (2000), 'Shifting the Margins: Black Feminist Perspectives on Discourses of Mothers in Child Sexual Abuse', in J. Radford, M. Friedberg and L. Harne (eds), *Women, Violence and Strategies for Action*, Open University Press, Buckingham, pp 103-19.

Birns, B. and Meyer, S. L. O. (1993), 'Mothers' Role in Incest: Dysfunctional Women or Dysfunctional Theories?', *Journal of Child Sexual Abuse*, Vol.2, No 3, pp. 127-35.

Boushel, M. (2000), 'What Kind of People are We? "Race", Anti-Racism and Social Welfare', *British Journal of Social Work*, Vol. 30, No 1, pp.71-89.

Boushel, M. and Lebacq, M. (1992), 'Towards Empowerment in Child Protection Work', *Children and Society*, Vol. 6, No 1, pp. 38-50.

Bradley, E. J. and Lindsay, R. C. L. (1987), 'Methodological and Ethical Issues in Child Abuse Research', *Journal of Family Violence*, Vol. 3, pp. 239-55.

Breckenridge, J. and Baldry, E. (1997), 'Workers dealing with Mother-Blame: in Child Sexual Assault Cases', *Journal of Child Sexual Abuse*, Vol. 6, No. 1, pp. 65-80.

Breckenridge, J. and Berreen, R. (1992), 'Dealing with Mother-Blame: Workers' Response to Incest and Child Sexual Abuse', in J. Breckenridge and M.

Carmody (eds), *Crimes of Violence: Australian Responses to rape and Sexual Assault*, Allen and Unwin, Sydney, pp.97-108.

Briere, J. and Runtz, M. (1993), 'Childhood Sexual Abuse: Long-Term Sequelae and Implications for Psychological Assessment', *Journal of Interpersonal Violence*, Vol. 8, No 3, pp. 312-30.

Browne, A. and Finkelhor, D. (1986), 'Impact of Child Sexual Abuse. A Review of the Research', *Psychological Bulletin*, Vol. 99, No 1, pp. 66-77.

Bryan, A. (1992), 'Working with Single Black Mothers: Myths and Reality', in L. Doyal and M. Langan (eds), *Women, Oppression and Social Work*, Routledge, London, pp. 169-85.

Bryan, B., Dadzie, S. and Scarfe, S. (1985), *The Heart of The Race: Black Women's Lives in Britain*, London, Virago.

Burstow, B, (1992), *Radical Feminist Therapy*, Newbury Park, CA, Sage.

Butt, J. and Mirza, K. (1998), *Social Care and Black Communities*, HMSO, London.

Cammaert, L. P. (1988), 'Non-offending Mothers: A New Conceptualisation', in L. E. A.Walker (ed), *Handbook on Sexual Abuse of Children*, New York, Springer, pp. 309-325.

Caplan, P. J. (1990), 'Making Mother-Blaming Visible: The Emperor's New Clothes', in J. Price Knowles and E. Cole (eds), *Woman-Defined Motherhood*, Harrington Park Press, Binghamton, New York, pp. 61-70.

Caplan, P.J. (1998), 'Mother-Blaming', in M. Ladd-Taylor and L. Umansky (eds), *"Bad" Mothers: The Politics of Blame in Twentieth-Century America*, New York University Press, New York, pp. 127-144.

Caplan, P. J. (2000), *The New: Don't Blame Mother: Mending the Mother-Daughter Relationship*, New York, Routledge.

Carby, H. (1992), 'White Women Listen! Black Feminism and the Boundaries of Sisterhood', in *The Empire Strikes Back: Race and Racism in 70s Britain*, Centre for Contemporary Cultural Studies, Race and Politics Group, Hutchinson, London, pp. 212-35.

Carter, B. (1993), 'Child Sexual Abuse: Impact on Mothers', *Affilia*, Vol. 8, No 1, pp. 72-90.

Chand, A. (2000), 'The Over-Representation of Black Children in the Child Protection System: Possible Causes, Consequences and Solutions', *Child and Family Social Work*, Vol. 5, No 1, pp. 67-77.

Channer, Y. and Parton, N. (1988), 'Racism, Cultural Relativism and Child Protection', in Violence Against Children Study Group (eds), *Taking Child Abuse Seriously*, Unwin Hyman, London, pp. 105-120.

Chigwada-Bailey, R. (1997), *Black Women's Experiences of Criminal Justice: A Discourse on Disadvantage*, Winchester, Waterside Press.

Cooper, A. (2000), 'Desire and the Law', in U. McCluskey and C. A. Hooper (eds), *Psychodynamic Perspectives on Abuse: The Cost of Fear*, Jessica Kingsley, London, pp. 243-62.

Corby, B. (1996), 'Risk Assessment in Child Protection Work', in H. Kemshall and J. Pritchard (eds), *Good Practice in Risk Assessment and Risk Management*, London, Jessica Kingsley, pp. 13-30.

Corby, B. (1998), *Managing Child Sexual Abuse Cases*, Jessica Kingsley Publishers Ltd, London.

Crenshaw, K. (1994), 'Mapping the Margins: Intersectionality, Identity Politics and Violence against Women of Colour', in M. A. Fineman and R. Mykitiuk (eds), *The Public Nature of Private Violence*, Routledge, New York, pp. 93-118.

Deblinger, E., McLeer, S.V., Atkins, M.S.D., Ralphe, E. and Foa, E. (1989), 'Post Traumatic Stress in Sexually Abused, Physically Abused and Non-Abused Children', *Child Abuse and Neglect*, Vol. 13, pp. 403-08.

Dempster, H. (1993), 'The Aftermath of Child Sexual Abuse: Women's Perspectives', in L. Waterhouse (ed), *Child Abuse and Child Abusers*, London, Jessica Kingsley, pp. 58-71.

DeYoung, M. (1994), 'Immediate Maternal Reactions to the Disclosure or Discovery of Incest', *Journal of Family Violence*, Vol. 9, No 1, pp. 21-33.

Dodson, J. (1975), *To Define Black Womanhood: A Study of Black Female Graduate Students*, The Institute of the Black World, Atlanta, GA.

DOH (1989), *An Introduction to the Children Act*, HMSO, London.

DOH (1995), *The Challenge to Partnership*, HMSO, London.

DOH (2000), Department for Education and Employment and Home Office, *The Framework for the Assessment of Children in Need and their Families*, The Stationery Office, London.

Dominelli, L. (1988), *Anti-Racist Social Work*, Macmillan, London.

Dove, N. (1998), *Afrikan Mothers: Bearers of Culture, Makers of Social Change*, State University of New York Press, New York.

Driver, E. (1989), 'Introduction', in E. Driver and A. Droisen (eds), *Child Sexual Abuse: Feminist Perspectives*, Macmillan, London, pp. 1-57.

Droisen, A. (1989), 'Racism and Anti-Semitism', in E. Driver and A. Droisen (eds), *Child Sexual Abuse: Feminist Perspectives*, London, Macmillan, pp. 158-69.

Elbow, M. and Mayfield, J. (1991), 'Mothers of Incest Victims: Villians, Victim, or Protectors?', *Families in Society*, Vol. 72, pp.78-84.

Erooga, M. and Print, B. (2000), 'Assessing Parental Capacity when Intrafamilial Sexual Abuse by an Adult is a Concern', in J. Horwath (ed), *The Child's World: Assessing Children in Need*, Department of Health, London, pp. 235-48.

Falberg, V. (1982), *Child Development*, London, BAAF.

Faller, K. C. (1988), 'The Myth of the Collusive Mother', *Journal of Interpersonal Violence*, Vol. 3, pp. 190-6.

Family Rights Group/NCH (1996), *Child Protection Enquiries: Mothers Talk About Their Families Experience*, Video.

Farmer, E. and Owen, M. (1995), *Child Protection Practice: Private Risks and Public Remedies – Decision Making, Intervention and Outcome in Child Protection Work*, HMSO, London.

Farmer, E. and Owen, M. (1996), 'Child Protection in a Multi-Racial Context', *Policy and Politics*, Vol 24, No 3, pp.299-313.

Farmer, E. and Owen, M. (1998), 'Gender and the Child Protection Process', *British Journal of Social Work*, Vol. 28, No 4, pp. 545-64.

Feiring, C., Taska, L., Lewis, M. (1996), A Process Model for Understanding Adaptation To Sexual Abuse: The Role of Shame in Defining Stigmatization, *Child Abuse and Neglect*, Vol. 20, No 8, pp. 767-82.

Fernando, S. (1995), 'Social Realities and Mental Health' in S. Fernando (ed), *Mental Health in a Multi-Ethnic Society*, Routledge, London, pp.11-35

Few, A. L. (1999), 'The (Un)making of Martyrs: Black Mothers, Daughters, and Intimate Violence', *Mothering and Motherhood*, Vol. 1, No 1, pp. 68-75.

Fonow, M. M. and Cook, J.A. (1991), 'Back to the Future: A Look at the Second Wave of Feminist Epistemology and Methodology', in M.M. Fonow and J.A. Cook (eds), *Beyond Methodology: Feminist Scholarship as Lived Research*, Indiana University Press, Indiana, pp. 1-15.

Finkelhor, D. (1986), *A Source of Child Sexual Abuse*, Sage, Beverley Hills, CA.

Garvey, N., Florence, J., Pezaro, S. and Tan, J. (1990), 'Mother-Blaming, the Perfect Alibi: Family Therapy and the Mothers of Incest Victims', *Journal of Feminist Therapy*, Vol. 2, pp. 1-25.

Geffner, R., Rosenbaum, A. J. and Hughes, H. (1988), 'Research Issues Concerning Family Violence', in V.B. Van Hassett, R.L. Morrison, A.S. Bellack and M. Hersen (eds), *Handbook of Family Violence*, Plenum, New York, pp.

Genero, N.P. (1998), 'Culture Resiliency and Mutual Psychological Development', in. H. McGubbin, E.A. Thompson, A.I. Thompson, and J. A. Futrell (eds), *Resiliency in African-American Families*, Sage, Thousand Oaks, CA, pp. 31-48.

Ghate, D. and Spencer, L. (1995), *The Prevalence of Child Sexual Abuse in Britain*, HMSO, London.

Gibbons, J., Conroy, S. and Bell, C. (1995), *Operating the Child Protection System: A Study of Child Protection Practices in English Local Authorities*, HMSO, London.

Gilgun, J. F. (1984), 'Does the Mother Know? Alternatives to Blaming Mothers for Child Sexual Abuse', *Response*, Vol. 7, pp. 2-4.

Glaser, B. G. and Strauss, A.L. (1976), *The Discovery of Grounded Theory*, Chicago, Aldine Press.

Glaser, D. and Frosh, S. (1988), *Child Sexual Abuse*, Macmillan, Gomes-Schwartz, B., Horowitz, J.M. and Cardarelli, A.P. (1990), *Child Sexual Abuse: The Initial Effects*, London, Sage.

Green, J. (1996), 'Mothers in Incest Families', *Violence Against Women*, Vol. 2, No 3, pp. 322-48.

108

Greene, B. (1990), 'Sturdy Bridges: The Role of African-American Mothers in the Socialisation of African-American Children', *Women and Therapy*, Vol.10, Nos 1-2, pp. 205-25.

Hammersley, M. (1996), 'The Relationship Between Qualitative and Quantitative Research: Paradigm Loyalty versus Methodological Eclecticism', in J.T.E. Richardson (ed), *Handbook of Qualitative Research Methods for Psychology and the Social Science*, Biddles Ltd, Leicester, pp. 159-74.

Hammersley, M. and Atkinson, P. (1995), *Ethnography: Principles in Practice*, London, Routledge.

Herzberger, S. H. (1993), 'The Cyclical Pattern of Child Abuse: A Study of Research Methodology', in C. M. Renzetti and R. M. Lee (eds), *Researching Sensitive Topics*, Sage, Newbury Park, CA, pp. 33-51.

Hester, M and Pearson, C. (1998), *From Periphery to Centre: Domestic Violence in Work with Abused Children*, The Policy Press, Bristol.

Hester, M., Pearson, C. and Harwin, N. (1998), *Making an Impact: Children and Domestic Violence*, Barnado's/NSPCC.

Hildebrand, J. (1989), 'Groupwork with Mothers of Sexually Abused Children', in W. Stainton Rodgers and E. Ash (eds), *Child Abuse and Neglect*, Batsford, London, pp. 244-45.

Hill Collins, P. (1990), *Black Feminist Thought*, Unwin Hyman, Inc, Massachusetts.

Hill Collins, P. (1997), 'The Meaning of Motherhood in Black Culture and Black Mother/Daughter Relationships', in M. M. Gergen and S. H. Davis (eds), *Toward a New Psychology of Gender*, Routledge, New York, pp. 325-40.

Hill Collins, P. (1998), *Fighting Words: Black Women and the Search for Justice*, University of Minnesota Press, Minneapolis, MN.

Hill, S.A. and Sprague, J. (1999), 'Parenting in Black and White Families: The Interaction of Gender with Race and Class', *Gender and Society*, Vol.13, No 4, pp. 480-499.

Hollies, L. A. (1990), 'A Daughter Survives Incest: A Retrospective Analysis', in E. C. White (ed), *Black Women's Health Book: Speaking For Ourselves*, Seal Press, Seattle, pp. 82-91.

hooks, b. (1994), *Outlaw Culture: Resisting Representations*, Routledge, London.

hooks, b (1995), *Killing Rage: Ending Racism*, Henry Holt and Co. Inc, New York.

hooks, b. (2000), *All About Love*, William Morrow and Co Inc, New York.

Hooper, C.A. (1992), *Mothers Surviving Sexual Abuse*, Routledge, London.

Hooper, C. A. (1997), 'Child Sexual Abuse and the Regulation of Women: Variations on a Theme', in L. L. O'Toole and J. R. Schiffman (eds), *Gender Violence: Interdisciplinary Perspectives*, New York University Press, New York, pp. 336-55.

Hooper, C. A. and Humphreys, C. (1997), 'What's in a Name: Reflections on the Term 'Non-Abusing Parent''', *Child Abuse Review*, Vol. 6, pp. 298-303.

Hooper, C.A. and Humphreys, C. (1998), 'Women whose Children have been Sexually Abused: Reflections on a Debate', *British Journal of Social Work*, Vol. 28, No 4, pp. 565-80.

Hooper, C. A. and Koprowska, J. (2000), 'Reparative Experience or Repeated Trauma? Child Sexual Abuse and Adult Mental Health Services', in U. McCluskey and C. A. Hooper (eds), *Psychodynamic Perspectives on Abuse: The Cost of Fear*, Jessica Kingsley, London, pp. 118-131.

Hudson, A. (1992), 'The Child Sexual Abuse Industry and Gender Relations in Social Work', in M. Langan and L. Day (eds), *Women Oppression and Social Work: Issues of Anti-Discriminatory Practice*, Routledge, London, pp. 129-41.

Humphreys, C., Atkar, S. and Baldwin, N. (1999), 'Discrimination in Child Protection Work: Recurring Themes in Work with Asian Families', *Child and Family Social Work*, Vol. 4, pp. 283-91.

Irwin, H. J. (1996), 'Traumatic Childhood Events, Perceived Availability of Emotional Support, and the Development of Dissociative Tendencies', *Child Abuse and Neglect*, Vol. 20, No 8, pp.701-7.

Jackson, S. and Tuson, G. (1999), 'Mothers' Involvement in Child Sexual Abuse Investigations and Support: Community Care or Child Protection?', in C. Bagley and K. Mallick (eds), *Child Sexual Abuse and Adult Offenders: New Theory and Research*, Ashgate, Aldershot, pp. 235-51.

Jackson, V. (1996), *Racism and Child Protection: The Black Experience of Child Sexual Abuse*, Cassell, London.

Jacobs, J. L. (1990), 'Reassessing Mother Blame in Incest', *Signs*, Vol. 15, pp. 500-14.

Jacobs, J. L. (1994), *Victimised Daughters: Incest and the Development of the Female Self*, Routledge, London.

James, J. (2000), 'Radicalising Feminism', in J. James and T. D. Sharpley-Whiting (eds), *The Black Feminist Reader*, Blackwell Publishing Inc, Massachusetts, pp. 239-58.

Johnson, J.T. (1992), *Mothers of Incest Survivors: Another Side of the Story*, Indiana University Press, Indianapolis, IN.

Jones, A. (1994), 'Anti-Racist Child Protection', in T. David (ed), *Protecting Children From Abuse: Multi-Professionalism and the Children Act*, Trentham Books Ltd, Stoke on Trent, pp. 25-37.

Joseph, G. (1991), 'Black Mothers and Daughters: Traditional and New Perspectives', in B. Guy-Sheftall, M. DeCosta-Willis, J. J. Royster, P. B. Bell-Scott, J. Sims-Wood and L. P. Fultz (eds), *Double Stitch: Black Women Write About Mothers and Daughters*, Harper Collin, New York, pp. 94-106.

Joyce, P. A. (1999), 'Clinical Social Workers Constructions of Mothers' Reactions to Children's Incest Disclosure', *Paper presented at the 6th International Family Violence Research Conference*, New Hampshire, USA.

Kelly, L. (1996), 'When does the Speaking Profit us: Reflections on the Challenges of Developing Feminist Perspectives on Abuse and Violence by Women', in M. Hester, L. Kelly and J. Radford (eds), *Women, Violence and Male Power*, Open University Press, Buckingham, pp. 35-49.

Kelly, L., Reagan, J. and Burton, S. (1994), 'Researching Women's Lives or Studying Women's Oppression? Reflections of What Constitutes Feminist Research', in M. Maynard and J. Purvis (eds), *Researching Women's Lives from a Feminist Perspective*, Taylor and Francis, London, pp.27-48.

Kelly, L., Reagan, L. and Burton, S. (1998), 'Making Connections – Building Bridges: Research into Action – Ten Years of the Child and Woman Abuse Studies Unit', in *The British Journal of Social Work*, Vol. 28, No 4, pp. 601-13.

Kinard, E. M. (1985), 'Ethical Issues in Research with Abused children', *Child Abuse and Neglect*, Vol. 9, pp. 301-11.

Kinard, E.M. (1994), 'Methodological Issues and Practical Problems in Conducting Research on Maltreated Children', *Child Abuse and Neglect*, Vol. 18, No 8, pp. 645-656.

King, E. (1996), 'The Use of Self in Qualitative Research', in J.T.E. Richardson (ed), *Handbook of Qualitative Research Methods for Psychology and the Social Sciences*, Biddles Ltd, Leicester, pp. 175-188.

Krane, J. and Davies, L. (2000), 'Mothering and Child Protection Practice: Rethinking Risk Assessment', *Child and Family Social Work*, Vol. 5, No 1, pp. 35-45.

Lawrence, E. (1992), 'In the Abundance of Water the Fool is Thirsty: Sociology and Black pathology', in *The Empire Strikes Back: Race and Racism in 70s Britain*, Centre for Contemporary Cultural Studies, Race and Politics Group, Hutchinson, London, pp. 94-142.

Lee, R. (1993), *Doing Research on Sensitive Topics*, Sage, London.

Levanthal, J.M. (1982), 'Research Strategies and Methodologic Standards in Studies of Risk Factors for Child Abuse', *Child Abuse and Neglect*, Vol. 6 pp. 113-23.

Lewis, G. (1996), 'Situated Voices: Black Women's Experience and Social Work', *Feminist Review*, Vol. 53, pp. 24-56.

Luthera, M. (1997), *Britain's Black Population: Social Change, Public Policy and Agenda*, Arena, Aldershot.

MacLeod, M. and Saraga, E. (1988), 'Challenging the Orthodoxy: Towards a Feminist Theory and Practice', *Feminist Review*, Vol. 32, No 2, pp. 30-49.

Maitra, B. (1995), 'Giving Due Consideration to the Family's Racial and Cultural Background', in P. Reder and C. Lucey (eds), *Assessment of Parenting: Psychiatric and Psychological Contributions*, London, Routledge, pp. 151-68.

Mama, A. (1993), 'Black Women and the Police: A Place Where the Law is not Upheld', in W. James and C. Harris (eds), *Inside Babylon: The Caribbean Diaspora in Britain*, Verso, London, pp. 135-51.

Mama, A. (1995), *Beyond The Mask: Race, Gender and Subjectivity*, Routledge, London.

Mama, A. (1996), *The Hidden Struggle: Statutory and Voluntary Sector Responses to Violence Against Black Women in the Home*, Whiting and Birch Ltd, London.

Marshall, A. (1994), 'Sensuous Sapphires: A Study of the Social Construction of Black Female Sexuality', in M. Maynard and J. Purvis (eds), *Researching Women's Lives from a Feminist Perspective*, Taylor and Francis, London, pp. 106-24.

Mauther, M. (1997), 'Methodological Aspects of Collecting Data from Children: Lessons from Three Research Projects', *Children and Society*, Vol. 11, pp. 16-28.

Mayall, B. (1991), 'Researching Child Care in a Multi-Ethnic Society', *New Community*, Vol. 17, No 4, pp. 553-68.

Maynard, M. and Purvis, J. (1994), *Research Women's Lives from a Feminist Perspective*, Taylor and Francis, London.

McAdoo, H.P. (1998), 'African-American Families: Strengths and Realities', in H.I. McGubbin, E.A. Thompson, A.I. Thompson and J.A. Futrell (eds), *Resiliency in African-American Families*, Sage, Thousand Oaks, CA, pp. 17-30.

McGubbin, H.I., Futrell, J.A., Thompson, E.A. and Thompson, A.I. (1998), 'Resilient Families in and Ethnic and Cultural Context', in H.I. McGubbin, E.A. Thompson, A.I. Thompson and J.A. Futrell (eds), *Resiliency in African-American Families*, Sage, Thousand Oaks, CA, pp. 329-51.

McIntre, K. (1981), 'Roles of Mothers in Father-Daughter Incest: A Feminist Analysis', *Social Work*, Vol. 26, pp. 462-6.

Mercer, K and Julien, I. (1988), 'Race, Sexual Politics and Black Masculinity: A Dossier', in R. Chapman and J. Rutherford (eds), *Male Order: Unwrapping Masculinity*, London, Lawrence and Wishart, pp. 97-148.

Miller, A. C. (1990), 'The Mother-Daughter Relationship and the Distortion of Reality in Childhood Sexual Abuse', in R. J. Perelberg and A. C. Miller (eds),*Gender and Power in Families*, Routledge, London, pp. 137-48.

Milner, J. (1993), 'A Disappearing Act: the Differing Career Paths of Fathers and Mothers in Child Protection Investigations', *Critical Social Policy*, Vol. 38, pp. 48-63.

Milner, J. (1996), 'Men's Resistance to Social Workers', in B. Fawcett, B. Featherstone, J. Hearn and C. Toft (eds), *Violence and Gender Relations: Theories and Interventions*, Sage, London, pp. 115-29.

Mittler, H. (1997), 'Core Groups: a Key Focus for Child Protection Training', *Social Work Education*, Vol. 16, No 2, pp. 77-91.

Moran-Ellis, J. (1995), 'Close to Home: The Experience of Researching Child Sexual Abuse', in M. Hester, L. Kelly, and J. Radford (eds), *Women, Violence and Male Power*, Open University Press, Buckingham, pp. 176-87.

Morris, A. (1999), Adding Insult to Injury, *Trouble and Strife*, No 40, pp. 30-5.

Mtezuka, M. (1996), 'Issues of Race and Culture in Child Abuse', in B. Fawcett, B. Featherstone, J. Hearn and C. Toft (eds), *Violence and Gender Relations: Theories and Interventions*, Sage, London, pp. 171-77.

Munro, E. (1998), 'Improving Social Workers' Knowledge Base in Child Protection Work', *British Journal of Social Work*, Vol. 28, pp. 89-105.

Myer, M. B. (1985), 'A New Look at Mothers of Incest Victims', *Journal of Social Work and Human Sexuality*, Vol. 3, pp. 47-58.

Nelson, S. (1987), *Incest: Fact and Myth*, 2nd ed, Stramullion Co-op Ltd, Edinburgh.

Nelson, S. (1998), 'Time to Break Professional Silences', *Child Abuse Review*, Vol. 7, pp. 144-153.

O'Hagan, K. (1997), 'The Problem of Engaging Men in Child Protection Work, *British Journal of Social Work*, Vol. 27, pp. 25-42.

O'Hagan, K. (1999), 'Culture, Cultural Identity and Cultural Sensitivity in Child and Family Social Work', *Child and Family Social Work*, Vol. 4, No 4, pp. 269-81.

O'Hagan, K. and Dillenburger, K. (1995), *The Abuse of Women Within Child Care Work*, Open University Press, Buckingham.

Oko, J. (2000), 'Towards A New Model of Practice', in P. Cox, S. Kershaw and J. Trotter (eds), *Child Sexual Assault: Feminist Perspectives*, Palgrave, Basingstoke, pp. 163-81.

Pajaczkowska, C. and Young, L. (1992), 'Racism, Representation, Psychoanalysis', in, J. Donald and A. Rattansi (eds), *'Race' Culture and Difference*, Sage, London, pp. 198-219.

Parker, R. (1997), 'The Production and Purposes of Maternal Ambivalence', in W. Holloway and B. Featherstone (eds), *Mothering and Ambivalence*, Routledge, London, pp. 17-36.

Parton, N. (1996), 'Social Work, Risk and 'The Blaming System', in N. Parton (ed), *Social Theory, Social Change and Social Work*, Routledge, London, pp. 98-114.

Parton, N. (1997), 'Child Protection and Family Support: Current Debates and Future Prospects', in N. Parton (ed), *Child Protection and Family Support: Tensions, Contradictions and Possibilities*, Routledge, London, pp. 1-14.

Parton, N. (1998), 'Risk, Advanced Liberalism and Child Welfare: The Need to Rediscover Uncertainty and Ambiguity', *British Journal of Social Work*, Vol. 28: pp. 5-27.

Patton, M. Q. (1990), *Qualitative Evaluation and Research Methods*, 2nd ed. Sage, Newbury Park, CA.

Peters, S. D. (1988), 'Child Sexual Abuse and Later Psychological Problems', in G. E. Wyatt and G. J. Powell (eds), *Lasting Effects of Child Sexual Abuse*, Sage, Newbury Park, CA, pp. 101-17.

Phillips, M. (1995), 'Issues of Ethnicity and Culture', in K. Wilson and A. James (eds), *The Child Protection Handbook*, Bailliere Tindall, London, pp.108-26.

Phoenix, A. (1990), 'Theories of Gender and Black Families', in T. Lovell (ed), *British Feminist Thought*, Basil Blackwell Ltd, Oxford, pp. 119-33.

Phoenix, A. (1994), 'Practising Feminist Research: The Intersection of Gender and "Race" in the Research Process', in M. Maynard and J. Purvis (eds), *Researching Women's Lives From a Feminist Perspective*, Taylor and Francis, London, pp. 49-71.

Pierce, R. and Pierce, L. (1987), 'Child Sexual Abuse: A Black Perspective', in R.L. Hampton (ed), *Violence in the Black Family*, Lexington, Lexington, MA, pp. 67-85.

Pigeon, N. and Henwood, K. (1996), 'Grounded Theory: Practical Implications', in, J. T. E. Richardson (ed), *Handbook of Qualitative Research Methods for Psychology and the Social Sciences*, Biddles Ltd, Leicester, pp. 86-101.

Pringle, K. (1998), 'Current Profeminist Debates Regarding Men in Social Welfare: Some National and Transnational Perspectives', *British Journal of Social Work*, Vol. 28, No 4, pp. 623-33.

Print, B. and Dey, C. (1992), 'Empowering Mothers of Sexually Abused Children a Positive Framework', in A. Bannister (ed), *From Hearing to Healing: Working with the Aftermath of Child Sexual Abuse*, Longman, London, pp. 55-81.

Reay, D. (1996), 'Insider Perspective or Stealing the Words out of Women's Mouth: Interpretation in the Research Process', *Feminist Review*, Vol. 53, pp. 57-73.

Reinharz, S. (1992), *Feminist Methods in Social Research*, Oxford University Press, New York.

Renzetti, C. (1997), 'Confession of a Reformed Positivist: Feminist Participatory Research as Good Social Science', in M. D. Schwartz (ed), *Researching Sexual Violence Against Women: Methodological and Personal Perspectives*, Sage, Thousand Oaks, CA, pp. 131-43.

Reynolds, T. (1997), '(Mis)representing the Black Superwoman', in H. S. Mirza (ed), *Black British Feminism*, Routledge, London, pp. 97-112.

Ribbens, J. and Edwards, R. (1998), 'Living on the Edges: Public Knowledge, Private Lives, Personal Experience', in J. Ribbens and R. Edwards (eds), *Feminist Dilemmas in Qualitative research*, Sage, London, pp. 1-23.

Richie, B. E. (1996), *Compelled to Crime: The Gender Entrapment of Battered Black Women*, Routledge, New York.

Roberts, H. (1981), *Doing Feminist Research*, London, Routledge and Kegan Paul.

Robinson, L. (1995), *Psychology for Social Workers: Black Perspectives*, Routledge, London.

Robinson, T. and Ward, J. V. (1991), 'A Belief in Self for Greater than Anyone's Disbelief: Cultivating Resistance Among African-American Female Adolescent', *Women and Therapy*, Vol. 2. Nos 3-4, pp. 87-104.

Rowan, A. B. and Foy, D. W. (1992), 'Posttraumatic Stress Disorder in Child Sexual Abuse Survivors: A Literature Review', *Journal of Traumatic Stress*, Vol. 6, pp. 3-20.

Rowan, A. B., Foy, D. W., Rodriguez, N. and Ryan, S. (1994), 'Posttraumatic Stress Disorder in a Clinical Sample of Adults Sexually Abused as Children', *Child Abuse and Neglect*, Vol. 18, pp. 51-61.

Russell, D. E. H. (1983), 'The Incidence and Prevalence of Intrafamilial and Extrafamilial Sexual Assault of Female Children', *Child Abuse and Neglect*, Vol. 7 pp. 133-46.

Russell, D.E.H. (1984), 'The Prevalence and Seriousness of Incestuous Abuse: Stepfathers vs Biological Fathers', *Child Abuse and Neglect*, Vol. 8, pp.15-22.

Russell, D.E.H. (1986), *The Secret Trauma: Incest in the Lives of Girls and Women*, Basic Books, New York.

Salt, P. (1990), 'Selection of the Treatment Sample', in B. Gomes-Schwartz, J. M. Horowitz and A. P. Cardarelli (eds), *Child Sexual Abuse: The Initial Effects*, Sage, Newbury Park, CA, pp. 43-56.

Salt, P., Myer, M., Coleman, L., and Sauzier, M. (1990), 'The Myth of the Mother as "Accomplice" to Child Sexual Abuse', in B. Gomes-Schwartz, J. M. Horowitz and A. P. Cardarelli (eds), *Child Sexual Abuse: The Initial Effects*, Sage, Newbury Park, CA, pp.109-31.

San Miguel, S.K., Morrison, G.M., Weissglass, T. (1995), 'The Relationship of Sources of Support and Service Needs: Resilience Patterns in Low-Income Latino/Hispanic Families', in H.I. McGubbin, E.A. Thompson, A.I. Thompson and J.Y. Fromer (eds), *Resiliency in Ethnic Minority Families: Native and Immigrant American Families*, University of Wisconsin System, Madison, WI, Vol. 1, pp. 49-70.

Saunders, B.E., Villeponteaux, L.A., Lipovsky, J.A., Kilpatrick, D.G. and Veronen, L.J. (1992), 'Child Sexual Assault as a Risk Factor for Mental Disorders Among Women', *Journal of Interpersonal Violence*, Vol. 7, pp. 189-204.

Schwartz, M.D. (1997), 'Emotion in Researching Violence Against Women', in M.D. Schwartz (ed), *Researching Sexual Violence Against Women: Methodological and Personal Perspectives*, Sage, Thousand Oaks, CA, pp. 71-73.

Scott, D.A. (1996), 'Parental Experiences in Cases of Child Sexual Abuse: A Qualitative Study', *Child and Family Social Work*, 1996, Vol. 1, pp. 107-14.

Seale, C. (1998), 'Qualitative Interviewing', in C Seale (ed), *Researching Society and Culture*, Sage, London, pp. 202-16.

Sharland, E., Jones, D., Aldgate, J., Seal, H. and Crocher, M. (1995), *Professional Interventions in Child Sexual Abuse*, HMSO, London.

Sinason, V. (2000), 'The Abuse of Learning Disabled People: Living and Working with the Consequences', in U. McCluskey and C. A. Hooper (eds),

Psychodynamic Perspectives on Abuse: The Cost of Fear, Jessica Kingsley, London, pp. 186-93.

Sirles, E. A. and Frank, P. J. (1989), 'Factors Influencing Mothers' Reactions to Intrafamily Sexual Abuse', *Child Abuse and Neglect*, Vol. 13, pp. 131-9.

Sgroi, S. M. and Dana, N. T. (1982), 'Individual and Group Treatment of Mothers of Incest Victims', in S. Sgroi (ed), *Handbook of Clinical Intervention in Child Sexual Abuse*, Lexington Books, Lexington, MA, pp. 191-214.

Skinner, J. (1998), 'Research as a Counselling Activity? A Discussion of Some Uses of Counselling Within the Context of Research on Sensitive Issues', *British Journal of Guidance and Counselling*, Vol. 26, No 4, pp. 533-40.

Skinner, J. (2000), *Coping with Survivors and Surviving*, Jessica Kingsley, London.

Smith, G. (1994), 'Parent, Partner, Protector: Conflicting Role Demands for Mothers of Sexually Abused Children', in M. Morrison and R. C. Beckett (eds), *Sexual Offending Against Children*, Routledge, London, pp. 179-202.

Smith, G. (1995), 'Hierarchy in Families Where Sexual Abuse is an Issue', in C. Burch and B. Speed (eds), *Gender, Power and Relationships*, Routledge, London, pp. 86-99.

Smith, V. (1998), *Not Just Race, Not Just Gender: Black Feminist Reading*, Routledge, New York.

Spacarelli, S. and Kim, S. (1995), 'Resilience Criteria and Factors Associated with Resilience in Sexually Abused Girls', *Child Abuse and Neglect*, Vol. 19, No 9, pp. 1171-82.

Staples, R. (1994), 'Family Structure: The Conflict Between Family Ideology and Structural Conditions', in R. Staples (ed), *The Black Family: Essays and Studies* (5th ed), Wadsworth, Belmont, CA, pp. 11-19.

Strauss, A. (1987), *Qualitative Analysis for Social Scientists*, Cambridge University Press, New York.

Strauss, A. and Corbin, J. (1990), *Basics of Qualitative Research*, Sage, Newbury Park, CA.

Surrey, J. L. (1991), 'Mother-Blaming and Clinical Theory', in J. Price Knowles and E. Cole (eds), *Woman-Defined Motherhood*, Harrington Press, Binghamton, New York, pp. 83-7.

Taylor, S. J. and Bogdan, R. (1984), *Introduction to Qualitative Research: The Search for Meanings* (2nd ed), John Wiley, New York.

Thanki, V. (1994), 'Ethnic Diversity and Child Protection', *Children and Society*, Vol. 8, No 3, pp. 232-44.

Thoburn, J., Lewis, A. and Shemmings, D. (1995), *Paternalism or Partnership? Family Involvement in Child Protection Process*, HMSO, London.

Thomas, L. K. (2000), 'What Cost Assimilation and Integration? Working with Transcultural Issues', in U. McCluskey and C. A. Hooper (eds), *Psychodynamic Perspectives on Abuse: The Cost of Fear*, Jessica Kingsley, London, pp. 118-31.

Thompson, E.A., McCubbin, H.I., Thompson, A.I and J.E. Fromer (eds), *Resiliency in ethnic minority families: Native and immigrant American families*, University of Wisconsin System, WI, Vol. 1, pp.385-400.

Thornton, C.I. and Carter, J.H. (1986), 'Treatment Considerations with Black Incestuous Families', *Journal of the National Medical Association*, Vol. 78, No l, pp. 49-53.

Trinder, L. (2000), 'Postmodern Feminism and the 'doing' of Research', in B. Fawcett, B. Featherstone, J. Fook and A. Rossiter (eds), *Practice Research in Social Work: Postmodern Feminist Perspectives*, Routledge, London, pp. 39-61.

Trotter, J. (1997), 'The Failure of Social Work Researchers, Teachers and Practitioners to Acknowledge or Engage Non-abusing Fathers: a Preliminary Discussion', *Social Work Education*, Vol. 16, No 2, pp. 63-76.

Trotter, J. (1998), *No One's Listening: Mothers, Fathers and Child Sexual Abuse*, Whiting and Birch Ltd, London.

Trowell, J. and Bower, M. (1995), *The Emotional Needs of Young Children and Their Families*, Routledge, London.

Truesdell, D. L., McNeil, J. S. and Deschner, J. P. (1986), 'Incidence of Wife Abuse in Incestuous Families', *Social Work*, Vol. 31, pp. 138-40.

Villarosa, L. (1994), *Body and Soul: The Black Women's Guide to Physical Health and Emotional Well-Being*, Harper Perennial, New York.

Walton, P. (1999), 'Empowerment: From Service Users to Service Providers', *Practice*, Vol. 11, No 1, pp. 5 –14.

Wattenberg, E. (1985), 'In a Different Light: A Feminist Perspective on the Role of Mothers in Father-Daughter Incest', *Child Welfare LXIV*, pp. 203-11.

West, T. C. (1999), *Wounds of Spirit: Black Women, Violence, and Resistance Ethics*, New York University Press, New York.

Westcott, H. (1996), 'Practising Ethical and Sensitive Child Protection Research', *Practice*, Vol. 8, No. 4, pp. 25-32.

Westcott, H. and Cross, M. (1996), *This Far and No Further: Towards Ending the Abuse of Disabled Children*, Birmingham, Venture Press.

Wheeler, E. (1994), 'Doing Black Mental Health Research: Observations and Experiences', in H. Afshar and M. Maynard (eds), *The Dynamics of 'Race' and Gender: Some Feminist Intervention*, Taylor and Francis, London, pp. 41-62.

Williams, C. (1999), 'Connecting Anti-Racism and Anti-Oppressive Theory and Practice: Retrenchment or Reappraisal?', *British Journal of Social Work*, Vol. 29, pp. 211-30.

Wilson, M. (1993), *Crossing the Boundaries: Black Women and Incest*, Virago, London.

Wolfe, D. A., Sas, L. and Wekerle, C. (1994), 'Factors Associated with the Development of Posttraumatic Stress Disorder Among Child Victims of Sexual Abuse', *Child Abuse and Neglect*, Vol, 18, pp. 37-50.

Wyatt, G. E. (1997), *Stolen Women: Reclaiming Our Sexuality, Taking Back Our Lives*, John Wiley and Sons, Inc, New York.

Wyatt, G. E. (1990), 'Sexual Abuse of Ethnic Minority Children: Identifying Dimensions of Victimisation', *Professional Psychology Research and Practice*, Vol. 21, No 5, pp. 338-43.

Wyatt, G. E. and Mickey, M.R. (1988), 'The Support by Parents and Others as it Mediates the Effects of Child Sexual Abuse', in G.E. Wyatt and G. Johnson Powell (eds), *The Long Lasting Effects of Child Sexual Abuse*, Sage, Newbury Park, CA, pp. 211- 25.

Index

120

121

123

124